The
Jesus
Generation

Dwight K. Nelson

HART RESEARCH CENTER
FALLBROOK, CALIFORNIA

Edited by Ken McFarland
Cover design by Ria Fisher
Cover illustration by Nathan Greene

ISBN 1-878046-24-1

Dedication

When I think of the snowy bearded patriarchs of old
  Who were the unabashed friends of God,
    I think of my grandfather, Ralph S. Watts, Sr.
Through the eighty-eight years of his sojourn across this
  planet
    As missionary preacher and church administrator,
He has lived out before his family and church and world
  A tenacious faith and a vibrant hope
    In a soon-coming Savior.

Though his eyes have grown dim,
  His faith has not.
    It will remain a shining legacy from him
      To those of us privileged to call him Grandpa.

He has passed on the torch of his fiery hope—
  So this book is dedicated to him and the dream
    He taught us to dream: The soon return of Jesus.

Contents

Preface

"JESUS IS COMING OCTOBER 28!" The bold newsprint headlines on the giant advertisement in *USA Today* leaped off the page: "JESUS WILL COME! OCTOBER 28 '92."

I did the quick arithmetic. The date on the newspaper was October 7, 1992. Which meant that according to this ad, there were only twenty-one days left—only three weeks until Jesus would come!

I'd be less than candid if I didn't confess that for this fifth-generation "adventist" heart, steeped in the tradition of a soon-coming Savior, reading that large one-and-a-quarter-inch headline became more than a casual act of curious perusal. After all, I belong to a community of faith that defines itself most passionately in the context of a mission to alert this dying planet to the glad news that Jesus IS coming soon. But who on earth would resort to buying that much ad space in *USA Today* to get the message out? And all for October 28, 1992?

After its arresting headline, the ad went on to quote 1 Thessalonians 5:4—"But you, brothers, are not in darkness so that this day should surprise you like a thief." Then underneath came a smaller warning—"WATCH OUT!"—and this list of "signs":

"Returning of millions Jewish people to home land. (Isa. 43:6)

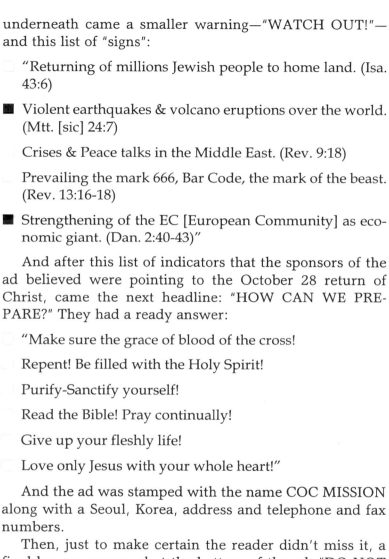 Violent earthquakes & volcano eruptions over the world. (Mtt. [sic] 24:7)

Crises & Peace talks in the Middle East. (Rev. 9:18)

Prevailing the mark 666, Bar Code, the mark of the beast. (Rev. 13:16-18)

Strengthening of the EC [European Community] as economic giant. (Dan. 2:40-43)"

And after this list of indicators that the sponsors of the ad believed were pointing to the October 28 return of Christ, came the next headline: "HOW CAN WE PREPARE?" They had a ready answer:

"Make sure the grace of blood of the cross!

Repent! Be filled with the Holy Spirit!

Purify-Sanctify yourself!

Read the Bible! Pray continually!

Give up your fleshly life!

Love only Jesus with your whole heart!"

And the ad was stamped with the name COC MISSION along with a Seoul, Korea, address and telephone and fax numbers.

Then, just to make certain the reader didn't miss it, a final banner appeared at the bottom of the ad: "DO NOT RECEIVE THE MARK 666, BAR CODE ON THE FOREHEAD OR RIGHT HAND!" Anyone who's read the Apocalypse recognizes the familiar symbolic imagery of Revelation 13. So is this it? Is this the fulfillment of the Apocalypse's great and shining hope?

Whoever they were, here was a group of Christians headquartered in Korea, with an apparent smattering at least of a global following, announcing the urgent warning that Jesus was coming in three weeks. So what was I, a reader of their proclamation, supposed to do?

I suppose I would have chuckled out loud were it not for the fact that my own spiritual roots and religious heritage are entwined with another, much more distant, group of Christians who also sacrificed their reputations to the ridicule of a mocking public. For they, too, believed that Jesus was coming in October. They, too, printed it in their newspapers and preached it from their street corners. Only the date they had calculated was October 22. One hundred forty-eight years earlier than these Koreans—1844.

And their disappointment must have been equally as great. Of the Korean hopeful, the Associated Press reported on October 29, 1992:

> Disillusioned worshipers attacked preachers today who had led them to believe that doomsday would come. Most leaders of the Seoul-based Mission for the Coming Days church, which had predicted that Wednesday [October 28] would bring the beginning of the end of the world, said their timing had been wrong. Police said church leaders could be charged with fraud. Some of the church's estimated 20,000 believers, many of whom had left their jobs or sold homes to prepare for the expected end of the world, reacted angrily. After doomsday services ended early today, worshipers threw hymn books at one preacher, cornered and slapped another and pulled one from his pulpit and beat him, Korean media reported. (*The Herald-Palladium*, October 29, 1992.)

Let's face it—nobody likes to be wrong. Nobody likes to be fooled. Nobody likes to live with disappointed hopes and illusionary dreams.

The followers of William Miller in 1844 were no exception. Their crushing grief over Jesus' "failure" to return as they had predicted is poignantly chronicled in Francis Nichols' history of their movement, *The Midnight Cry*. From the diary of Hiram Edson, one of Miller's followers, appears this tear-stained entry, describing the moments after midnight's last toll on October 22, 1844:

> Our fondest hopes and expectations were blasted, and such spirit of weeping came over us as I never experienced before. It seemed that the loss of all earthly friends could have been no comparison. We wept, and wept, till the day dawn. I mused in my own heart, saying, My advent experience has been the richest and brightest of all my Christian experience. If this had proved a failure, what was the rest of my Christian experience worth? Has the Bible proved a failure? Is there no God, no heaven, no golden home city, no paradise? Is all this but a cunningly devised fable? Is there no reality to our fondest hope and expectation of these things? And thus we had something to grieve and weep over, if all our fond hopes were lost. And as I said, we wept till the day dawn. (pp. 247, 248.)

Just an isolated aberration? Hardly. Listen to how another shattered Christian described the cruel reality of having to live on with only the shards of a broken hope:

> That day came and passed, and the darkness of another night closed in upon the world. But with that darkness came a pang of disappointment to the advent believers that can find a parallel only in the sorrow of the disciples after the crucifixion of their Lord. The passing of the time was a bitter disappointment. True believers had given up all for Christ, and had shared His presence as never before. The love of Jesus filled every soul; and

with inexpressible desire they prayed, 'Come, Lord Jesus, and come quickly'; but He did not come. And now, to turn again to the cares, perplexities, and dangers of life, in full view of jeering and reviling unbelievers who scoffed as never before, was a terrible trial of faith and patience. When Elder Himes visited Waterbury, Vt., a short time after the passing of the time, and stated that the brethren should prepare for another cold winter, my feelings were almost uncontrollable. I left the place of meeting and wept like a child. (Ibid.)

A band of disappointed Millerites a century and a half ago, a church of disappointed Koreans a few months ago—what can we possibly have in common with such an odd and strange conglomeration of apocalyptic has-beens? After all, you and I are certainly more sophisticated intellectually, are we not? Who could possibly dupe us into the cardinal sin of date setting anymore? Oh sure, the Millerite movement was indeed the progenitor of the now-global Adventist movement. But we're much brighter and wiser and a whole lot less vulnerable, aren't we?

October 22, October 28—we fall for neither. And in fact, if someone studied our personal theological and eschatological convictions today, no doubt the date a lot of us have settled for is the twelfth. The twelfth of never.

Oh, none of us is foolish enough to articulate such a conviction. And no doubt if we were pressed with the query—Do you believe Jesus is coming soon?—we would answer with rote precision as seven generations before us have answered: Why, of course! But rote responses, with their stale and musty certainties, are hardly adequate anymore, are they? And besides, there is a world of difference between lipping our advent hope and living it.

So one can't help but quietly admire the sheer courage of the Millerites and the Koreans who have lived out their hopes—irrespective of their prophetic blunders.

As for the Koreans, I had all but forgotten about their

October 28 prediction when that Wednesday morning dawned. While I was shaving, I was listening to an all-news radio station out of Chicago, when the morning anchor matter-of-factly announced that a group of people was holed up inside some church in the Windy City. It appears, he went on, that they expect Jesus Christ to return today.

The words cut right through the lather straight to my heart: JESUS CHRIST TO RETURN TODAY. And to hear it announced with such matter-of-fact candor over the radio! Here I am, getting prepped for another busy day of life as an Adventist—a day about my parish not much different from the one that preceded it and probably little different from the one that will follow. And there they are—whoever they are—holed up in a church at a prayer service, all because today is the day they expect Jesus to return! What a painfully stark contrast between expectations.

But of course I was right, and they were wrong.

Then again, in an irrefutable way, could it be that in being wrong, they were also right? Not in their calculations, but in their commitment? Not in their exegesis, but in their expectancy? Maybe their story is to be repeated yet again.

Maybe there will yet come a generation of men and women and children on this planet who really will live unabashedly and unashamedly with the pulsating expectancy that Jesus is soon to come. Not only Koreans, but Africans and Europeans and Asians and Americans south and north. A final generation of human beings on earth—the last generation in this civilization's history, a generation whose personal *and* public headlines will proclaim the glad tidings: JESUS IS COMING SOON!

That such a Jesus Generation will exist at the terminus of time is clear enough from the pages of the Apocalypse. Revelation 13 describes the apocalyptic showdown marking the end of earth's rebellion. In the view of many Bible expositors from diverse religious communions, that final global and spiritual showdown will be precipitated as God's end-time people faithfully proclaim the Three Angels' Messages of Revelation 14:6-12—God's last appeal to a dying planet. Given our understandable preoccupation with the climactic messages of the three angels, could we inadvertently overlook the shining portrayal of God's last generation chronicled in the preceding verses? When was the last time you reflectively mused on this radiant portrait?

> Then I looked, and there was the Lamb, standing on Mount Zion! And with him were one hundred forty-four thousand who had his name and his Father's name written on their foreheads. And I heard a voice from heaven like the sound of many waters and like the sound of loud thunder; the voice I heard was like the sound of harpists playing on their harps, and they sing a new song before the throne and before the four living creatures and before the elders. No one could learn that song except the one hundred forty-four thousand who have been redeemed from the earth. . . . These follow the Lamb wherever he goes. They have been redeemed from humankind as first fruits for God and for the Lamb. (Revelation 14:1-4.)

Who are these people "redeemed from humankind," who "follow the Lamb wherever he goes"? The number 144,000 seems symbolically to represent a far more vast multitude, considering the figurative imagery that surrounds this group. If Revelation's description of the 144,000 were taken literally in every respect, then they would have to be limited to unmarried male Jews who follow Jesus (see Revelation 7:4-8). And while Christ certainly does call for such followers today, the apocalyptic symbols are much richer than the limited applications such literal depictions would suggest.

Wedged as it is between the final showdown in Revelation 13 and the second coming of Christ in chapter fourteen, it is abundantly clear that in sweeping strokes, John paints on his apocalyptic canvas a portrait of the end-time generation—of all the followers of Christ. Let them be called the Jesus Generation, for these are they who "follow the Lamb wherever he goes." What a powerful portrayal!

The very Jesus who was lifted up on that crimson Roman stake as the Lamb of God—this same Jesus is the passion and pursuit of this end-time generation. He is not only their victorious Savior; He is their triumphant Lord. "They follow the Lamb." For when you know that Calvary's nailed-open, wide-open embrace is God's outstretched offer for you—for you personally, for you alone—how can you not help but gratefully follow the Savior wherever He leads you? The Jesus Generation follows.

But it is more than a mindless, rote following that John splashes across this canvas. For he paints this generation with two names upon their foreheads: the name of the Lamb and the name of the Father. Can you fathom that? Here is a generation of contemporary men and women, old and young, that is known across the face of this planet for the twin symbols of divine ownership and character. Why, it's practically written across their faces and upon their lives: I belong to the Father; I belong to the Lamb!

There are some of us who have hesitated to get personalized license plates for our cars, simply because we ruefully concede that if we were to put our names on those plates, we'd have to be a lot more careful about the way we drive! Come on, now—be honest. You may choose a clever nickname or some ingenious byline for your plates, but there aren't a lot of drivers who want to go on public record in traffic with their own names blazoned on their licenses!

But not so with the Jesus Generation. John airbrushes the very names of the Father and the Lamb onto the countenances of this end-time people. A generation that moves up the crowded alley-ways and down the sophisticated thoroughfares of human society with the shining Name above all names painted across their lives.

But 1,900 years after John's canvas work, what can it possibly mean for us to live the life of the Jesus Generation in our very contemporary contexts? Is it even possible any more?

What follows in this book is a quest for the answer. Because October 22, 1844, and October 28, 1992, have come and gone. And we are still here. Jesus hasn't come. Yet.

But I believe the "yet" is much closer than any of us dares to realize! In my book *Countdown to the Showdown*, the forerunner to this present volume, I undertook a comparative study of the prophetic events of the Apocalypse, juxtaposed with some of the global events of the year 1992. And I came to the unequivocal conviction that we have entered this planet's final showdown with destiny. The advent of Christ is much nearer than we have previously thought. I reaffirm that belief at the outset of this second book. And with even greater certainty.

I cannot speak for the Koreans of October 28, 1992, for they are only a news story to me. But my life is bound up with that apocalyptic movement that, like a phoenix, rose out of the ashes of the Millerite disappointment nearly a century and a half ago. It is a movement that would do well to embrace and heed the confession of that aging Baptist preacher who had for so long championed the proclamation of a soon-coming Jesus. On November 10, 1844, less than three weeks after the Great Disappointment, William Miller penned these words in a letter to a dejected colleague and friend:

> Hold fast; let no man take your crown. I have fixed my mind upon another time, and here I mean to stand until God gives me more light.— And that is *Today*, TODAY, and TODAY, until He comes, and I see HIM for whom my soul yearns. (Emphasis Miller's in Nichol, p. 267.)

"Today, today, and today, until He comes." Therein is

the fiery context within which the Jesus Generation must live. No wonder John ended his apocalyptic painting with the prayer, "Even so, come, Lord Jesus." For it is the flame of that resplendent hope that must ignite the minds and hearts and souls and lives of the Jesus Generation.

That you, reader, have been called to be a part of that generation is a glad certainty. And that this book might become an open door to a deepening walk with the Jesus of that generation is my quiet hope and prayer.

Dwight K. Nelson
New Year's Day, 1993
Pioneer Memorial Church
at Andrews University

Acknowledgments

For a decade now, I've had the privilege of pastoring the Pioneer Memorial Church here on the campus of Andrews University. Like *Countdown to the Show-down*, this sequel to that book grew out of a series of sermons to the students, faculty, and community members of this congregation. We have shared the journey together, and I am the one blessed because of their companionship.

Pastoring this campus has been both exhilarating and humbling. Exhilarating, because what can compare to the cutting-edge challenge of interacting with the minds of young scholars-to-be in their quest to know God? Humbling, because awash in a sea of exploding knowledge, I am constantly reminded of my own evident limitations in seeking to communicate to my parish a contemporary word from and about God. It has been their response to this series that has encouraged me to share it.

In preparing the manuscript for publication, I am again indebted to the kindness of two parishioner friends, Verna and Ed Streeter. Their editorial acumen and computer skills were a godsend. And I'm thankful for their partnership in ministry.

I'm also grateful for my friend and colleague in this pastorate, Skip MacCarty. His careful critique of the manuscript was invaluable. And his unselfish willingness to share his giftedness continues to energize my own ministry.

And to the Hart team, for whom this represents our fourth book together, my appreciative thanks. Dan Houghton, the publisher, has been both relentless in his vision and accommodating with his deadlines. And I'm glad. Ken McFarland, the editor, has graciously harnessed overnight mail and faxes to lend his expertise and encouragement. And I'm grateful.

And while it may not be customary for authors to mention the publisher's graphic designers, I want to acknowledge the artistic collaboration of Ria Fisher and Nathan Greene in the cover work of both *Countdown to the Showdown* and this book. The blending of her design with his masterful brush work has powerfully captured the themes of both books. And I thank them.

However, my deeper gratitude is for my three soulmates in this journey. It should have been enough for them to have to sit through this series with the rest of the congregation. But Kirk and Kristen went the second mile in cheerfully granting their dad some snowbound Christmas vacation hours to complete this manuscript. And my wife, Karen—whose love and friendship have been the unkept secret to my life and ministry from the start—has been my partner through it all. With my family, I am thrice blessed!

Finally, the Moravians long ago circumnavigated the globe for Jesus, heralding as their Latin motto—*Vicit agnus noster, eum sequamur.* Which, being interpreted, means, "Our Lamb has conquered; Him let us follow." Knowing what we know about this present moment in unfolding history, is it not the right hour to unfurl that crimson banner once again and let it snap in the windblown heavens of earth's final generation? One need not be Moravian to embrace that truth. It is enough to be a part of the Jesus Generation.

Vicit agnus noster, eum sequamur.

1

Life Goes On . . . and On . . . Or Does It?

L ast winter our little girl Kristin was carrying on a rather ponderous philosophical conversation with her mother. Krissy, who was five years old at the time, was still sorting out this "yesterday-today-tomorrow" delineation of time. And as she was being tucked into bed, out of the blue she asked, "Mommy, now that it's *tonight*, is this *tomorrow*?"

Well, come to think of it, that is a very probing question, isn't it? Logically, it makes sense to conclude that once it's toNIGHT, it can't be toDAY. And if tonight is not today, then is it tomorrow? When was the last time you wrestled with that one? Anyway, Kristin wanted to know.

Karen's quick reply was, "No, Kris, it's *not tomorrow*."

Looking up from her pillow, Kristin retorted, "Well, is it *yesterday* then?" Obviously, in five-year-old logic, if tonight is not today and not tomorrow, then it must be yesterday.

"No, sweetie, this is *today.*"

"Well, Mommy, then when does it become *tomorrow?*"

To which Karen replied, "When you wake up in the morning, it'll be *tomorrow.*"

Kristin thought long and hard for a moment, and then with perplexity written all over her puzzled face, she asked, **"Mommy, are we still ourselves?"**

It makes you wonder, doesn't it? Have we become so confused about time that we are no longer ourselves? You start out with a philosophical discussion of time and end up with the great ontological debate, Are we still ourselves? And all of that from a five-year-old. Maybe our children are wiser than we think!

For a century and a half now, people across this nation and around the earth have proclaimed the soon coming of Christ. Tomorrow is almost here, they have cried out! Today has almost become yesterday, and tonight is nearly tomorrow. So now before tonight becomes yesterday and tomorrow becomes today, it's time to get ready!

There is a name for a people with that kind of com-pressed understanding of time—Adventists. Men and women, young and aged, who still believe that Jesus is coming soon. In fact, the word you'll hear them use to describe His return is *imminent.* The dictionary offers this definition: an event often dangerous in nature, which is impending, threateningly, hanging over one's head, ready to befall or overtake one, close at hand in its incidence, coming on shortly.

"Coming on shortly"—do we believe that about Jesus' coming any more? You see, it may be that for many of us, my little girl's question presses rather closely, **Are we still ourselves?** Or have we become so confused about time that we're no longer ourselves any more, no longer our "advent-ist" selves? As a people who once believed in the imminence of Christ's return, in all this confusion of time, **are we still ourselves?**

Well, it's confusing, isn't it, being a generation that has had to grow up surrounded and saturated with the rampant and recurring signs of Christ's return and yet still not being certain about the end?

Look what the Jesus Generation has had to live through! Why, when you can lay them side by side, there's hardly a difference between the headlines of your evening paper and the red alert Jesus left for his end-time generation in Matthew 24:

> When he was sitting on the Mount of Olives, the disciples came to him privately, saying, "Tell us, when will this be, and what will be the sign of your coming and of the end of the age?" Jesus answered them, "Beware that no one leads you astray. For many will come in my name, saying, 'I am the Messiah!' and they will lead many astray. And you will hear of wars and rumors of wars; see that you are not alarmed; for this must take place, but the end is not yet. For nation will rise against nation, and kingdom against kingdom, and there will be famines and earthquakes in various places: all this is but the beginning of the birth-pangs. (Matthew 24:3-8.)

"Famines and earthquakes in various places." Read what the editors of *Time* magazine wrote at the disturbing end to a string of natural disasters this past summer:

> "Natural" is not a word that links logically with "disaster." But together the words emphasize how little control humans have over the events they describe. Almost without pause, nature lately has shattered, crushed and flooded the earth with a series of cataclysms that have killed hundreds, caused incalculable damage and left survivors shaken.
>
> On the same day in mid-August, a volcano erupted in Alaska, an earthquake hit near Alaska's

Andreanof Islands and another rocked Kyrgyzstan in the former Soviet Union. Two weeks ago, Hurricane Andrew hit the Bahamas, then ripped through Florida and Louisiana. Last week the chain of disasters continued. Tropical Storm Polly drenched eastern China and killed at least 150 people. Typhoon Omar, which had earlier raked Guam, headed for the Philippines. In Afghanistan flash floods swept through the valleys of the Hindu Kush, leaving hundreds dead or missing.

Probably the most spectacular of the week's calamities began with a major earthquake under the Pacific Ocean 30 miles off the west coast of Nicaragua. The temblor spawned tsunamis, commonly known as tidal waves, that towered as high as 45 ft. in spots and rolled over dozens of small towns along 200 miles of coast. Surging inland, the waves crushed houses and hotels and swept people out to sea. Nicaraguan civil defense officials said 116 were killed and 150 missing. (*Time*, September 14, 1992, p. 14.)

You aren't reading the summary of an itinerant evangelist. This is an alarmed recapitulation from savvy, crises-hardened journalists. You don't have to be a believer in much of anything any more in order to come to the unsettling conclusion that the meteorological balance of this planet has been terribly skewed.

An Associated Press release from Washington, D.C., on September 15, 1992, spoke of "an unprecedented string of natural disasters from Florida to Guam" that made the late-summer string "one of the worst runs of natural calamities in modern times." Quoting a colonel in the Salvation Army, the release continues: "'These cataclysmic events are almost Biblical in proportion.'" Almost biblical? Sobering reverberations from Matthew 24, to be sure.

The Associated Press was sufficiently impressed with the long-running string of calamities that inflicted our planet last year, that it issued the following September 27 headline: "GRAPHIC EVIDENCE, 1992: Year of natural disasters." Beneath that pronouncement in a boxed chart appeared a map of the world with numbered dots for twenty-three catastrophic disasters that struck our globe during the first nine months of 1992: avalanches, earthquakes, typhoons, volcanic eruptions, hurricanes, floods— all of them killers with their death statistics in tow.

And after that litany of twenty-three, there were still three months left to the year! Three months that meted out further disasters, among which were a killer quake in Cairo (1,000 estimated killed) and killer tsunamis in Indonesia (death toll estimated in the hundreds). Add to that the slow and living death of the Somalian famine and indeed the headlines accurately read "1992: Year of natural disasters." Somber echoes of Matthew 24.

But not just in the natural realm. Jesus warned of an exponential rise of upheavals in the political realm as well. "For nation will rise against nation, and kingdom against kingdom." And how about republic against republic? The continuing measured collapse within the republics of the former Soviet Union and their bloody civil wars are evidence enough that peace remains forever elusive on this terrestrial ball. And just when Europe was celebrating a *pax Europa* with the dismantling of the Berlin Wall and the collapse of Communism, a festering wound in the former Yugoslavian republics broke out into a ravaging cancer that threatens the very stability of that entire continent. Bosnia, Serbia, Croatia—the suppertime names of our evening news—now join the infamous hot spots of Israel, Palestine, Lebanon, Syria, Iraq, Ireland, Peru, Columbia, Cambodia, Sri Lanka, and South Africa.

But Jesus wasn't through. "And because of the increase of lawlessness, the love of many will grow cold" (verse 12). You can almost feel that love grown cold in the figures the FBI released in declaring juvenile crimes up 25 percent in the last decade. Violent crimes by people of all ages, the report went on, reached a record high last year—up 33 percent since 1982. "Increase of lawlessness" from a love grown cold. Why, it's the whole family values issue of the 1992 presidential campaign. But it's now desperately clear that family values are not merely a political issue for our nation; they are a moral dilemma for our planet!

How did Jesus put it? "All this is but the beginning of the birthpangs" (verse 8). Matthew 24's throbbing litany makes it clear that life on this planet will one day collapse upon itself! The economic disarray of the European Community is symptomatic of a global financial and economic hemorrhage. Notice this AP release, datelined London:

> The world is struggling through an economic malaise that shows no signs of ending any time soon, with all of the financial superpowers facing enormous difficulties that may well be beyond the control of mere politicians. The United States, the world's biggest economy, is staggering. Japan is spending billions in a bid to stimulate growth. Europe has been wrenched by a currency crisis that has threatened hopes for unity among its major nations. . . . During previous recessions, one of these great economic engines was running and able to pull the rest of the world out of the slump. Now, they are all sputtering. "It looks pretty grim, and one has to wonder how long we'll have to live in this gloomy environment," said Jim O'Neill, chief economist at Swiss Bank Corp. in London. (*South Bend Tribune*, September 20, 1992.)

I have read Larry Burkett's new book, *The Coming Economic Earthquake*. And whether or not you agree with his political ideology, you will find his economic case study of this nation's financial crisis compelling if not irrefutable. Burkett notes that our real national debt stands now at $6 trillion. Our government annually brings in approximately $1.4 trillion in income but is spending $1.8 trillion during the same twelve months. Anybody who can balance a checkbook knows that when you spend more than you earn, you're getting nowhere fast!

If our current trend of skyrocketing national indebtedness continues, the potential debt by the year 2000 will be between $13 and $20 trillion. And at the current 10 percent interest rate for the national debt, the interest payments alone on $13 trillion will be $1.3 trillion annually! And remember, we're currently bringing in only $1.4 trillion annually.

Listen to Burkett:

> Not only is [the federal deficit] out of control, there appears to be no rational voice in the capitol trying to straighten out the mess. I can't emphasize too strongly that the federal debt (as well as the private sector debt) can and will destroy our economy. . . . There never has been anything approaching this level of debt funding in the history of mankind in so short a period of time, even on a percentage basis. (p. 121.)

Politicians know that the only solution left to the problem would drive voters away by the droves—drastic spending cuts and sizable tax increases. Burkett's point is simply that, short of those radical interventions, we're headed straight into the heart of a national economic earthquake—a financial crisis before which the Great Depression of early this century will pale. And all the economic summits our new president might summon cannot stave the hemorrhaging.

Burkett is right. An author who wrote a century before he did predicted that national ruin and national apostasy would be inextricably linked: "This national apostasy will speedily be followed by national ruin." (*Last Day Events*, p. 134.) And if you've read Revelation 18 lately, you know that economic collapse is dramatically linked with the final apocalyptic showdown. International crisis and ruin (Revelation 18) will be linked with moral and spiritual apostasy (Revelation 13).

I can hear the strident voices now: Until our nation returns God to the classroom and the courtroom, we shall suffer His offended judgments! That isn't a direct quote, you understand. But here's one that is. Straight from the dais of a convocation of the Religious Right in Virginia Beach, Virginia, last fall comes this ominous linkage from Pat Robertson, one of the prominent voices in the burgeoning religious-political coaltion: "The recent major natural disasters—the San Francisco earthquake, Hurricane Andrew and Hurricane Iniki—are evidences that God is displeased with the wickedness of our nation. We can expect these disasters to increase until we get our nation back to God."

One wonders to what extent such voices might seek state enforcement of religion to somehow stave off the judgments of God and return this nation to divine favor!*

Jesus' description of the end and Revelation's prediction of the coalition that will bring it on make all the sense in the world when you're living in the world we live in right now! How can you live through these times and not conclude that Jesus is coming soon? And tomorrow is on the heels of today? **But, Mommy, are we still ourselves?**

Are we? In a quick tale at the end of Matthew 24, Jesus pointedly reminds us that *when you let go of tomorrow, you lose hold of today.*

> Who then is the faithful and wise slave, whom his master has put in charge of his household, to give the other slaves their allowance of food at the proper time? Blessed is that slave whom his master will find at work when he arrives. Truly I tell you, he will put that one in charge of all his possessions. But if that wicked slave says to himself,

---

*See my chapter, "Is the New Christian Right Wrong?" in *Countdown to the Showdown* for a more in-depth analysis of this coalition.

> "My master is delayed," and he begins to beat his fellow slaves, and eats and drinks with drunkards, the master of that slave will come on a day when he does not expect him and at an hour that he does not know. He will cut him in pieces and put him with the hypocrites, where there will be weeping and gnashing of teeth. (Matthew 24:45-51.)

Not exactly a bedtime story! But the Greek can also read that the master cuts the wicked slave *off,* rather than *up.* Obviously, Jesus isn't describing a dismemberment here, since the master assigns this servant a place with the hypocrites, where there is weeping and gnashing of teeth.

But more important than the fate of the servant is the philosophy of the servant—"I think I'll put tomorrow on hold; my master's been delayed; I may as well loosen up a bit and go for it all now; I mean, life goes on and on and on . . . " His theme song? "Let's forget about tomorrow, for tomorrow never comes!" And does he ever forget about tomorrow!

His boisterous and abusive neglect simply confirms that truth that **when you let go of tomorrow, you lose hold of today.** "And he begins to beat his fellow slaves, and eats and drinks with drunkards." (verse 49.) It's clear that he shouldn't have written tomorrow off so assuredly; for his hope of the future was in fact his help for the present.

Langdon Gilkey wrote the well-known *Shantung Compound* as a chronicle of his prison camp experience during World War II. Gilkey, a young American professor teaching in China at the outbreak of the war, was rounded up by the invading enemy along with other European expatriates and shipped by train to an inland prison camp known as Shantung Compound. His book is the tale of their ordeal in that crowded camp. Near the end of his book, Gilkey pens a line that describes how vital tomorrow is for our survival today:

> Only when destiny gives us the great gift of an open future are we able fully to live, for intense

life in the present is made up in large part of expectancy. Whenever we are alive and excited, it is
the future and not the past that enlivens the present moment. (p. 223.)

Did you catch that? "Intense life in the present is made
up in large part of expectancy."

Gilkey's right, isn't he? And that was precisely Jesus'
point, was it not? Our hope of tomorrow fires our hold on
today. That is what kept the first slave going in Jesus' story.
It was his expectancy of tomorrow that gave such vitality
for today. Not so his unfortunate colleague, who in letting
go of tomorrow, lost hold of today as well.

Intensity is created by expectancy. Show me a man or a
woman who is ignited by the hope of tomorrow, and I'll
show you somebody who is passionately in touch with
today—living it with daring and energy.

And that is what the advent hope is all about! Jesus is
coming soon! That is the single tomorrow that must shape
our every today. "Blessed is that slave whom his master will
find at work when he arrives."

I know that there are some who soft-pedal our hope in
tomorrow by the casual observation that—Hey, life goes on
and on and on . . . so what does it matter if Jesus comes
tomorrow or if He comes in 100 years? All that matters is
that He's coming, right?

Wrong! Fritz Guy masterfully disassembles that line of
reasoning in the book *Pilgrimage of Hope*, where he wrote
that it is quite odd for someone to suggest that it doesn't
matter if Christ comes next week or the next decade or the
next century. That, he writes, would be like saying, "I don't
care if I get married next week or next year or in ten years
. . . as long as I eventually get married!" Guy concludes,
Either that person is revealing an appalling ignorance of the
nature of marriage, or he evidences an incredible lack of
love!

That would be like living in enemy-held territory (Shantung Compound) and declaring that it doesn't matter if liberation comes this decade or next, as long as it comes! If I'm living in the land of the enemy, you can be certain that I long to be liberated ASAP!

"Even so, come, Lord Jesus." I want out of here! Which is why Adventism must continue to refuse to let go of His promised tomorrow. For it is that very expectancy that shapes the intensity with which Jesus calls the Jesus Generation to live out their todays.

Let go of tomorrow, and you'll lose hold of today.

"Blessed is that slave whom his master will find at work when he arrives."

And by the way, Jesus isn't calling you to slave for Him—but to gladly live for Him. This is what the Jesus Generation is all about.

A Kentucky Fried Chicken sign reads: "Thank you for coming. Please return soon." A 1990s version of the Apocalypse's, "Even so, come, Lord Jesus." When that becomes our daily prayer, then **we are still ourselves**—the Jesus Generation.

2

The Kingdom of Heaven Is Like Unto Gatorade

Because the kingdom of heaven is like unto Gatorade, I wish there were a way for me to transform this page into a video monitor. Then you'd be able to view for yourself the Gatorade television commercial that contains the secret to the kingdom of heaven.

Not that you have to be a great fan of this salty drink of the athletes. I'm not. But if all the advertising hype has a fraction of truth to it, then Gatorade really does have the capacity to replenish some of the body's electrolytes and sodium expended during vigorous exercise. Which is no small feat, I suppose. And which is why you'll often see the prominent display of this highly touted beverage at major sporting events.

You may even witness some poor, hapless coach having an entire canister of Gatorade dumped over him from behind, if he's lucky enough to be coaching the winning team that day!

But back to the kingdom of heaven. And Michael Jordan. Because Michael Jordan happens to be the star of the Gatorade commercial in question. Now, in the event you're no more an avid fan of professional basketball than you are of Gatorade, let me hasten to explain that Michael Jordan plays for the Chicago Bulls and is nearly unanimously considered to be the greatest superstar in the history of basketball. (I say it's nearly unanimous, because you may happen to be like my teenage son, who believes those accolades belong to Isiah Thomas of the Detroit Pistons.) Jordan, you may remember, was also the basketball star of the much-heralded U.S. Olympic Dream Team at the '92 Barcelona Games.

So the producers of Gatorade (which happen to be the Quaker Oats Company—now you know why oatmeal and Gatorade have about the same amount of taste appeal!) knew what they were doing when they signed Michael Jordan to an advertising contract. And what they produced with his help became a very clever, catchy commercial.

In rapid-fire sequence, the commercial begins with live action shots of young boys and girls, older youth, and even some grownups—all shooting hoops and playing basketball, all trying very hard to imitate Michael Jordan. You can tell they're trying to copy him by the trademark way they hold their tongues (Jordan's is usually partially extended when he races in for a shot with the basketball), or by the way they try to execute their layups, or by their attempts at fancy mid-air shots.

But just in case the viewer isn't sure, the commercial plays a song that keeps singing, "I want to be like Mike." Over and over the words are sung as the back-lot shots are made, "I want to be like Mike, I want to be like Mike."

To punctuate the ad with an exclamation point, near the close of the ad, big white letters flash against a jet-black background: Be like Mike, Be like Mike, Be like Mike. And the final picture of the commercial is a shot of Michael Jordan, the great superstar himself, grinning and drinking—you guessed it—Gatorade! (Anybody thirsty yet?)

The kingdom of heaven is like unto Gatorade. Because God has a commercial, too. And it also repeats, Be like Mike, Be like Mike. Or rather, Be like Michael, Be like Michael . . . the Michael of the Apocalypse (Revelation 12:7), the Jesus of the Incarnation (Jude 9, 1 Thessalonians 4:16). Which makes the kingdom of heaven like unto Gatorade. Because God has a song. And it goes, "Be like Jesus."

But who sings the song any more? After all, it's America's favorite pastime to spend its loose change trying be like Hollywood's glittering showcase of starlets and stars, isn't it? We'd rather be like Tom Cruise than Jesus Christ. And aren't we the nation that worships with punctual regularity at the weekend sports shrines of our million-dollar super jocks? Give us Jordan, not Jesus.

Don't our most hallowed temples line a Street called Wall? Aren't the inside traders of that cultic avenue America's revered? And as I write these words, we're all mimicking the dashing young Turks making the heady journey from Little Rock to the White House. Preoccupied with Clinton, who needs Christ?

In a world where the names and faces of the elite, the wealthy, the beautiful, the popular, the successful, and the powerful are the daily fare of our swooning media, isn't it a bit tacky to hoist the picture of Jesus, the humble Galilean? And isn't it a bit odd to talk of a *Jesus* Generation? Because let's face it. The average citizen has enough trouble trying to keep up with Joneses. So how can anyone possibly keep up with Jesus?

Hence, who needs a Jesus Generation?

A fair question, I suppose, considering the already overloaded and over-stressed world in which we live. But when you factor in the mounting evidence that earmarks this present generation as this earth's last, the question is neither trite nor redundant.

Who needs a Jesus Generation? God does.

You think about it for a moment. Knowing what you know about the contemporary human plight, why does God wait? What could He possibly be waiting for? Another earthquake or volcano or two, more mayhem and murder, a few more bloody wars or rapes or AIDS cases, or some other new scourge to wrack humanity? Is that it? Is that why Jesus hasn't returned yet? If so, how much worse would you say this planet has to get before He can return?

The fact of the matter is that our global systems—economic, political, social, ecological, and moral—are disintegrating faster than we humans can possibly repair them. The hole in earth's last dike is irreparable, its gaping mouth cracking wider and wider with each advancing headline. It's all about to come crashing in. God can hardly be waiting for planetary life to get any worse! If Jesus doesn't come soon, the entire organism will devour itself and die, which, by the way, is Lucifer's fondest dream.

So what is God's dream? Again, it makes all the sense in the world to wonder out loud, What's He waiting for?

Ask the Big Fisherman, and Peter is quick with a ready answer. God does have a dream alright, and He longs for its fulfillment. Call it the Gatorade dream, with you and me in the middle of it. You may read the dream for yourself at the end of that aging bit of a letter that Peter dashed to us shortly before he was crucified upside down—Rome's thankless reward to him for being a disciple of Jesus. Scrawled by the gnarly hands of the aging fisherman, 2 Peter 3 is an urgent summons to us who are jammed between the headlines of the impending end:

> Since all these things are to be dissolved in this way, what sort of persons ought you to be in leading lives of holiness and godliness, waiting for and hastening the coming of the day of God? (Verses 11, 12.)

That is, seeing that the end is near, what kind of people ought we to be who await the return of Christ? Or to put it in the query of the Christian philosopher Francis Schaeffer, "How then shall we live?"—we who live on the brink of eternity.

It's a pertinent inquiry, is it not? For we can count down to the showdown till we're blue in the face; **but if we aren't shaping up for the showdown, what good is it to get there?** The Jesus Generation is that generation of men and women, young and aged, who will get there. The question is, Are *we* among them? Will *we* get there?

The kingdom of heaven is like unto Gatorade. Be like Mike? No, *no*, NO! God says, Be like Me. In fact, that's precisely what God is saying through Peter when 2 Peter 3:11 uses the word *godliness*. Everyone knows that godliness is an abbreviation for God-like-ness—dropping the "k" and the "e" to shorthand it into godliness. Godliness, then, means to be like God. Which is also the literal meaning of the name Michael ("like God").

And what is God like? Peter knows. For he was there, crowded around that torchlit table, bread crumbs spilled across the white linen and the Passover chalice still wet with its purple juice. His feet washed clean by the strong hands of the Master, Peter leans over the table to hold the face of Jesus in his gaze and to catch the quiet assurances that breathed from the Master's lips that fated Thursday night in the upper room. In less than twelve hours, though Peter and the rest knew it not, Jesus would be dead, hung out to die on that crimson stake. But tonight it is the reassuring claim that Peter will never forget. Forever after, Peter would know what God is like. For hadn't Jesus spoken, "I and the Father are one; if you have seen Me, you have seen the Father also"? (John 10:30; 14:9.) And Peter would never—could never—forget that to be Godlike is to be Christlike. Godliness would forever after mean to be like Jesus.

Thus the inescapable question for all those who read Peter and know Jesus is: Are you, am I, like Jesus?

To be honest with you, I must confess that my wife and two kids know exactly how I should answer that question. And you may have a friend or spouse or roommate who's just as candid. But the question persists, Are you, am I, like Jesus?

Quite frankly, I'd feel a lot more comfortable if the query were changed to—Do you *want* to be like Jesus? If that were the question, what would be your reflective answer?

But it seems a wild hope and a foolish dream, doesn't it, this prayer to be like Jesus? That any contemporary survivor these days could ever possibly hope to be like Jesus has all the earmarks of an eternal long shot. But then again, if the odds were really as long as eternity, Peter's words would amount to little more than a spiritual taunt! If Peter is suggesting an impossibly high ideal, than all that his readers are left with is a pie-in-the-sky bit of euphemism that ends up a cruel ideal indeed! Especially if neither Peter nor God ever believed that godliness was possible, or that we could ever truly be like Michael, be like Jesus—like God.

But you certainly don't get that impression reading Peter! Why, his very inference suggests that Peter firmly believes godliness and holiness are the shining hallmark of an end-time generation. Read the end of his letter. With clarion certainty Peter portrays a generation living on this planet at the end of human civilization who will be God-like, who will be like Jesus!

The Jesus Generation. A global community of men and women and children who apparently draw so close to their Savior and Master that the onlooking universe sees the very character of Christ shining from their earthbound lives.

"Since everything will be destroyed in this way, what kind of people ought you to be? You ought to live holy and godly lives as you look forward to the day of God and speed its coming" (2 Peter 3:11, 12, NIV). Note the link Peter made between living godly lives, being like Jesus, and speeding His return.

If that sounds far-fetched to you, get hold of what Peter

suggests next: The sooner this end-time generation becomes like Jesus, the sooner will come the return of Jesus. It's right there in verse 12, where Peter speaks of our "waiting for *and hastening* the coming of the day of God" (emphasis supplied). Or as the New International Version translates it, "as you look forward to the day of God and *speed its coming*" (emphasis supplied). In the four other places this Greek word is used in the New Testament, it also carries the meaning, to hurry or to hasten.

By his juxtaposition of the words, "godliness" and "hasten," Peter intentionally and irrefutably links two vital elements that at the end of time become insepara- ble—**calendar** and **character**. "What sort of persons ought you to be in godliness [character], as you wait for and hasten the coming of Christ [calendar]?"

This is Peter's bombshell—developing the character of Christ will hasten the coming of Christ. And the apostle's implications are clear that calendar and character are to be inversely proportional, which means the less you have of one, the more you have the other. That is, the less we have of our calendar, the more we must have of Christ's charac- ter. Or, the closer we get to the end, the more we must become like our Friend.

But then, haven't we lived with this proposition for decades? Have you read this statement recently out of that classic on Jesus' parables, *Christ's Object Lessons?*

> Christ is waiting with longing desire for the mani-
> festation of Himself in His church. When the char-
> acter of Christ shall be perfectly reproduced in
> His people, then He will come to claim them as
> His own. It is the privilege of every Christian not
> only to look for but to hasten the coming of our
> Lord Jesus Christ. (Page 69.)

Did you catch again the notion that we can actually hasten the return of Jesus? There it is—the intentional linkage of calendar and character. Developing the character of Christ will hasten the coming of Christ. Ellen White's suggestion is that the calendar of time will run out for an end-time generation when the character of Christ shines out from the Jesus Generation. "When the character of Christ shall be perfectly reproduced in His people, then He will come to claim them as His own."

But I must hasten to add a caveat, lest these sentences become fodder for those troubled hearts prone to snatch every hint of human perfection and twist it to their own hurt. The context for both Peter and Ellen White's proposition is clear. Peter's opening salvo in his last letter rings with the truth about the Source of any and all human godliness: "May grace and peace be yours in abundance in the knowledge of God and of Jesus our Lord. *His divine power has given us everything needed for life and godliness*, through the knowledge of him who called us by his own glory and goodness" (2 Peter 1:3, emphasis supplied).

Peter is crystal clear! Jesus' divine power is the sole source of every bit of life and godliness any human heart possesses! Which means that the very quest to be like Jesus must be daily enabled by the presence and the power of Jesus.

Remember that long-ago line, "All His biddings are enablings" (Ibid., p. 333)? That is Peter's point. His proposal to be like Jesus ("godliness") is premised on the power that comes from Jesus. And whatever else you may call it, that is the gift of grace—grace full and free! "May grace be yours in abundance," Peter exclaims! Grace from beginning to end for the Jesus Generation. Which is why Peter repeats his beginning in his ending: "But grow in the grace and knowledge of our Lord and Savior Jesus Christ. To him be the glory both now and to the day of eternity. Amen" (2 Peter 3:18). Grace and peace and power for the Jesus Generation, all wrapped up in Jesus. "To him be the glory," indeed!

Ellen White is just as clear with her statement. Read the sentences that precede it, and it becomes evident that she too would direct our hearts to Him who is our grace and life. Using the imagery of plant life, she writes:

> The plant grows by receiving that which God has provided to sustain its life. It sends down its roots into the earth. It drinks in the sunshine, the dew, and the rain. It receives the life-giving properties from the air. *So the Christian is to grow by co-operating with the divine agencies. Feeling our helplessness. . . . we are to take deep root in Christ.* As the plant receives the sunshine, the dew, and the rain, we are to open our hearts to the Holy Spirit. . . . *By constantly relying upon Christ as our personal Saviour, we shall grow up into Him in all things who is our head.* . . . As you receive the Spirit of Christ—the Spirit of unselfish love and labor for others—you will grow and bring forth fruit. (Pages 66-68, emphasis supplied.)

Over and over, like Peter, she declares the empowering and enabling Source of human godliness and Christ-likeness to be Jesus. Only after she has thoroughly built that Jesus-centered construct does she conclude with the familiar words: "Christ is waiting with longing desire for the manifestation of Himself in His church. When the character of Christ shall be perfectly reproduced in His people, then He will come to claim them as His own" (p. 69).

No wonder God still waits. He can't be waiting for more signs to be fulfilled and the earth to grow worse; the planet is already set on self-destruct. Instead, God quietly waits with earnest longing to see the shining reflection of His own character of relentless love in the Jesus Generation. The great eschatological issue, as the theologians would put it, isn't about calendars; it's about character—the character of God reflected in the characters of an end-time generation. Then at last the universe shall behold a generation that will have "become a spectacle to the world, to angels and to mortals" (1 Cornithians 4:9)—a generation which has the name (signifying the divine character) of the Lamb and the name of the Father written upon their foreheads (Revelation 14:1).

It's no wonder Peter climaxes the last letter of his life with the impassioned appeal, "But grow in the grace and knowledge of our Lord and Savior Jesus Christ" (2 Peter 3:18). Because it is by beholding Him that we become changed into His likeness (see 2 Corinthians 3:18).* So if you want to be like Jesus, doesn't it make all the sense in the world to spend some quiet time every single day gazing into His life and learning of His character? Drink Gatorade if you want to be like Jordan; but read the gospels if you want to be like Jesus.

That's why I'd like to invite you to join me in a renewed spiritual pilgrimage.

At an Alamo Rental Car counter in Washington, D.C., recently, I met an Alamo agent who in the course of our conversation told me that he had become a Christian. Again. "I got it back!" he grinned at me.

"Got what back?" I questioned.

"You know, the Spirit. I got Him back. Used to be filled with Him, but I fell away." He lowered his voice so the others in the room wouldn't hear. "But I got Him now. And I plan to keep Him." He flashed another knowing grin.

This was my chance. "Listen, friend, I've got just the book for you. Because if you want to keep the Spirit of Jesus in your life, you're going to need to keep in touch with Jesus throughout your day. Give me your name and address, and I'll mail this book to you. I've read it many times myself, so I know it'll bless you, too."

The Alamo agent scribbled down the particulars, and I promised to have a copy of *The Desire of Ages* in the mail as soon as I got back to Michigan.

When I got back home, I got an extra copy of the book, jotted a note to the man, and sent it off in the mail. But the

---

*In my book *A New Way to Pray*, I have outlined a simple method of devotional praying that will enable you to utilize the great spiritual law of 2 Corinthians 3:18: "By beholding, we become changed."

reason I'm sharing this with you is that something came over me while I was standing by that stack of paperback copies of *The Desire of Ages*, leading me to pick one up for myself. Sure, I had the hardback edition back in my study. But with all the times I'd read it and marked it before, I decided that what I needed was a fresh new unmarked journey through a clean, unmarked copy of this classic on the life of Jesus. A chapter a morning—another vignette of the Master for each new day.

So it was that bright and early the next morning, I headed down to my basement study and pulled out my new copy of *The Desire of Ages* and began a fresh journey into the life of Jesus. Why? Because I really meant it when I suggested earlier in this chapter that for both you and me the greatest desire of all might be the prayer to be like Jesus.

Isn't that what the Jesus Generation lives for? "Be like Jesus, this my song, in the home and in the throng; be like Jesus all day long; I would be like Jesus."

By beholding Him, the Jesus Generation will become changed. Not according to Gatorade. But rather, according to God. For in the end, who wants to be like Jordan, when you can be like Jesus?

> *Be like Jesus,*
>   *This my song,*
> *In the home*
>   *And in the throng;*
> *Be like Jesus,*
>   *All day long;*
> *I would be like Jesus.*
>   *—James Rowe*

3

To Awaken the Dawn

The Wall Street Journal carried the story. Datelined Seoul, Korea, the news report detailed the account of a certain Lee Jang-Lim, whom the Korean government is charging with fraud and illegal possession of foreign currency. "Authorities allege that the 46-year-old Mr. Lee is deviously, not divinely, inspired" (October 6, 1992).

But inspired or not, he is obviously inspiring! The Journal reports that $628,000 in bank checks and bonds were found hidden in his house, along with $26,711 in U.S. currency. Authorities believe it is part of nearly $4.2 million in assets that thousands of Koreans have turned over to Mr. Lee and his church, The Dami Missionary Church. But government prosecutors doubt Mr. Lee "practices what he preaches."

The telltale evidence for such a conclusion was the fact that this minister was found to be holding bank certificates of deposit that mature in May 1993, which turns out to be long past the date on which he was predicting the world's end! Lee Jang-Lim, you see, was a major proponent of the "Jesus is coming on October 28, 1992" movement I referred to in the preface of this book. He preached Jesus' return on October 28, but carried CDs that wouldn't mature until May 1993. Just in case, perhaps. But still, something doesn't seem to quite add up, does it?

Listen to the sobs of one of his disillusioned followers—a broken-hearted mother the *Journal* quoted at the end of its report on the now publicly disgraced and discredited October 28 movement:

> "The government has got to think about what will happen after October 28 when nothing happens," says Lee Seung-Eun, the head of a group of alleged doomsdayer victims. Like others, she worries about mass suicide. Her son has left college to hide in the mountains with other doomsdayers to prepare for the seven-year war between good and evil that will follow the return of Jesus, as foretold in the Bible. "He is learning kickboxing to fight the Antichrist," she says tearfully. (Ibid.)

Learning how to kickbox in preparation for the end of time—there has got to be a better way! *The Wall Street Journal* was right that Mr. Lee was wrong. Jesus did not come on October 28, 1992. But the incontrovertible fact remains that He is coming soon!

How then shall we live—we who eagerly await that long-promised, oft-heralded moment? The Apocalypse leaves no question as to the answer. In describing the generation of men, women, and children who will be the last generation to live on this planet before Jesus' triumphant return, Revelation 14 portrays them as the ones who "hold fast to the faith of Jesus" (Revelation 14:12). That NRSV rendering of those familiar words is a powerful portrayal of the Jesus Generation—they are the ones holding fast to Jesus!

Holding fast to Jesus has neither to do with kickboxing

the Antichrist, or shadow boxing with it, for that matter! Holding fast to Jesus has to do with a generation of human beings whose "highest desire is to become more and more Christlike" (*Last Day Events*, p. 192). Here is an end-time people who long to be like Jesus.

But the inescapable query is, How? How can this generation, which you and I are called to be a part of, become like Jesus?

Let me share with you some "adventist" thoughts from a Baptist minister and philosopher who has written a book that has blessed and benefited me greatly. In *The Spirit of the Disciplines*, Dallas Willard, professor and past director of the School of Philosophy at the University of Southern California, shares a metaphor that provides the key to answering our how-to question. And he takes it from the world of sports.

Take America's favorite pastime of baseball, for example. Kids throughout the nation have no trouble picking out their sports heroes, thanks to all the media hype that accompanies professional sports in our country. Add to the quotient the thousands of kids who collect baseball cards, as my son does, and the fascination with the star athletes is only compounded. Of those kids, Dallas Willard writes:

> Think of certain young people who idolize an outstanding baseball player. They want nothing so much as to pitch or run or hit as well as their idol. So what do they do? *When they are playing in a baseball game*, they all try to behave exactly as their favorite baseball star does. The star is well known for sliding headfirst into bases, so the teenagers do, too. The star holds his bat above his head, so the teenagers do, too. These young people try anything and everything their idol does, hoping to be like him—they buy the type of shoes the star wears, the same glove he uses, the same bat. (Page 3, emphasis his.)

But then Willard pauses and asks the revealing question, Will these kids, after all their imitating, actually succeed in performing like the star? He responds as we all would:

> We all know the answer quite well. We know that they won't succeed if all they do is try to be like him in the game—no matter how gifted they may be in their own way. And we all understand why. The star performer himself didn't achieve his excellence by trying to behave in a certain way *only during the game.* Instead, he chose an overall life of preparation of mind and body, pouring all his energies into that total preparation, to provide a foundation in the body's automatic responses and strength for his conscious efforts during the game. (Pages 3, 4, emphasis his.)

So what does all this have to do with being the Jesus Generation? I mean, come on, we're not talking about baseball here. We're talking about end-time Christianity—a generation that wants to be like Jesus Christ, not Jose Canseco.

Let Willard continue for another moment:

> What we find here is true of any human endeavor capable of giving significance to our lives. We are touching upon a general principle of human life. It's true for the public speaker or the musician, the teacher or the surgeon. A successful performance at a moment of crisis rests largely and essentially upon the depths of a self wisely and rigorously prepared in the totality of its being— mind and body. (Ibid.)

Willard is right, isn't he? If you want to be like an outstanding individual in your own profession or career circles, you don't start by mimicking his or her public behavior—you begin by seeking to model his private discipline. The fact is that we all have people we have sought to emulate—men and women we've admired and looked up to. And often times unconsciously, we have said, I want to be like him, I want to be like her. But we all recognize that there isn't one of these individuals who became the success that he or she is without years of rigorous discipline and arduous training and daily practice.

Willard moves to his bottom line:

> This is not a truth to be set aside when we come to our relationship with God. We are saved by grace, of course, and by it alone, and not because we deserve it. That is the basis of God's acceptance of us. But grace does *not* mean that sufficient strength and insight will be automatically 'infused' into our being in the moment of need. Abundant evidence for this claim is available precisely in the experience of any Christian. We only have to look at the facts. A baseball player who expects to excel in the game without adequate exercise of his body is no more ridiculous than the Christian who hopes to be able to act in the manner of Christ when put to the test without the appropriate exercise in godly living. (Pages 4, 5, emphasis his.)

Did you catch that? "No more ridiculous than the Christian who hopes to be able to act in the manner of Christ . . . without the appropriate exercise in godly living," Willard exclaims!

And of course, Willard's right, isn't he? Being like Jesus has a whole lot to do with behaving like Jesus, to be sure. **But living like Jesus did in public has everything to do with living like Jesus did in private.** And that is Willard's bottom line: "To live as Christ lived is to live as he did *all* his life" (p. 5, emphasis his). The rest of *The Spirit of the Disciplines* is a masterful description of the spiritually disciplined life Jesus lived—the very life He calls His contemporary disciples like you and me to follow.

A life that in its soul center begins and ends with prayer. It was that way for Jesus. Some months ago as I was reading through the Gospel of Luke, I was intrigued by Luke's poignant and persistent portrayal of Jesus in prayer. In fact, I began to annotate his repeated references.

"But he would withdraw to deserted places and pray" (Luke 5: 16). Not once, not twice, but as Luke's choice of words indicates, it was on a repeated basis that Jesus sought the solitude of a prayer encounter with His Father. I like the way Arndt and Gingrich, the Greek lexicographers, translated this line: "He would steal away to the lonely places and pray." To steal away to pray—that was the practice of Jesus. One exceptional line from Luke? No, there are in fact seven such exemplary lines from the gospel writer.

Actually, the first mention of Jesus in prayer was as He dripped little pools of water all over the muddy banks of the Jordan River. He is kneeling before the gaping throng.

> Now when all the people were baptized, and when Jesus also had been baptized and was praying, the heaven was opened, and the Holy Spirit descended upon him in bodily form like a dove. (Luke 3:21, 22.)

A vignette of Jesus praying at His own baptism—a prayer that was continued for forty days and nights with fasting and solitude in the wilderness. Nearly six non-stop weeks of solitude and silence! Why, we'd go crazy if we attempted to do the same, wouldn't we? Or is it that we've gone crazy by not doing the same? I want to return to that thought in a moment.

Was the wilderness experience an aberration? Luke 5:16, as noted above, suggests not. Its reference to Jesus stealing away to a deserted place to pray also helps us understand the fuller meaning of Luke 4:42. Even though Luke doesn't use the words *to pray* in the latter verse, the implied intent is clear—"At daybreak he departed and went into a deserted place."

But there is more. "Now during those days he went out to the mountain to pray" (6:12).

Three chapters later, Luke describes the Master in prayer with His disciples: "Once . . . Jesus was praying alone, with only the disciples near him" (Luke 9:18).

But the gospel writer isn't finished portraying the prayer life of Jesus. "Now about eight days after these sayings Jesus took with him Peter and John and James, and went up on the mountain to pray" (9:28).

Over and over again, we can read Luke's persistent portrayal of Jesus in prayer. "He was praying in a certain place" (11:1).

And of course, there is Jesus' most famous prayer vigil of all in the Garden of Gethsemane: "Then he withdrew from them about a stone's throw, knelt down, and prayed, 'Father, if you are willing, remove this cup from me; yet, not my will but yours be done'" (Luke 22:41, 42).

There they are—seven prominent depictions of Jesus in prayer. What do you suppose the gospel writer is trying to tell us? Could it be that in Luke's intentional repetition we encounter the truth that being alone with God is the secret to being at one with God? **You can't be at one with Him, unless you're alone with Him.** Just look at Jesus . . . *look at Jesus!*

"But he would steal away to the lonely places and pray."

That's the problem, isn't it? Who's got any lonely places to steal away to any more? Crowded dorm rooms and crowded classrooms. Crowded bedrooms and crowded bathrooms. Crowded waiting rooms and crowded work rooms. Crowded offices and crowded premises. They're always there, the crowds. No wonder we can't steal away to a lonely place!

Or is it that we just keep bringing the crowds along? Thanks to Sony, that is. Do you remember the first radio your parents ever bought you and how they lived to regret it for the rest of their lives?

I was in third grade when Mom and Dad bought me a beautiful little Sony AM transistor radio. We were living in the land where Sonys were built, before the days when FM stations were popular, if you can believe that! I was so proud of that little black transistor radio with its round gold speaker box on the front.

With my earplug in, I used to crawl into bed at night and listen to the AFRTS (Armed Forces Radio and Television Service) station broadcasting in English there in Tokyo, Japan. And when I woke up, the first thing I'd do was switch on my radio.

One thoughtful little gift. And soon my world of silence was invaded and conquered—day and night—by a tiny electronic voice that was always with me.

"But he would steal away to the lonely places and pray." Why? Because being alone with God is the secret to being at one with God.

Maybe our problem isn't the lack of available lonely places; maybe it's the lack of making personal choices. Walkman, Watchman, AM, FM, CD, TV, in the car, on the plane, while we're eating, jogging, resting, working, playing, even while we're sleeping—we have no lonely place to go to, because we never go alone. The electronic voice is with us.

Some years ago I came across these words of that twentieth-century mystic, Thomas Merton:

> Those who love God should attempt to preserve
> or create an atmosphere in which he can be
> found. Christians should have quiet homes.
> Throw out the television, if necessary—not every-
> body, but those who take this sort of thing seri-
> ously. Radios are useless. Stay away from the
> movies—I was going to say 'as a penance,' but it
> would seem to me to be rather a pleasure than a
> penance to stay away. Let those who can stand a
> little silence find other people who like silence,
> and create silence and peace for one another.

When you gain this interior silence, you can carry
it around with you in the world, and pray every-
where. It is absurd to talk about interior silence
where there is no exterior silence. (*Leadership,*
summer 1981, p. 64.)

"But he would steal away to the lonely places and pray."
Why? Because being alone with God is the secret of being
at one with God. You can't be at one with Him, unless
you're alone with Him.

Seven times Luke describes Jesus leaving the crowds and
His closest companions behind in order to experience the
solitude and silence of communion with His Father. M. E.
Dodd, in his book *The Prayer Life of Jesus,* draws the
inescapable conclusion:

What a lesson for us poor mortals, teaching us
that if prayer is to be real and vital and intimate
there must be certain spots to which we can hide
ourselves away from the storms of life's temptations and trials for a season with the Good Father.
To us it may be some quiet spot on the old farm;
some little country church house; some invalid
chair; some attic corner in our own home; some
closet in our place of business; some secluded corner in the church house; some particular pew;
some place—any place where "God comes down
our souls to greet, and glory crowns the mercy
seat." (Page 25.)

And all in pursuit of God through solitude and silence—
the very disciplines Lucifer has masterfully eliminated from
our harried, hectic lives!

Richard Foster, in his book *Celebration of Discipline* is right:
"In contemporary society our Adversary majors in three
things: noise, hurry and crowds." No silence, no solitude.

And what is the result? Dallas Willard tells of experi-
ments conducted with mice and amphetamine. It took

twenty times more amphetamine to kill an individual mouse than to kill mice in groups. Experimenters found that if they placed an amphetimine-free mouse in the midst of a group of mice already on the drug, that poor, drug-free mouse would be dead within ten minutes! So strong was the erratic group behavior of the drugged mice ("In groups they go off like popcorn or firecrackers," is how Willard described them!), that the healthy mouse began to imitate the frenzied dysfunction of the group and eventually dropped over dead from trying to keep up with the drugged mice.

His point?

> Our conformity to social pattern is hardly less re-
> markable than that of the mice—and just as
> deadly. . . . In solitude, we purposefully abstain
> from interaction with other human beings, deny-
> ing ourselves companionship and all that comes
> from our conscious interaction with others. We
> close ourselves away. . . . Solitude frees us, actu-
> ally. This above all explains its primacy and prior-
> ity among the disciplines. The normal course of
> day-to-day human interactions locks us into pat-
> terns of feeling, thought, and action that are
> geared to a world set against God. Nothing but
> solitude can allow the development of a freedom
> from the ingrained behaviors that hinder our inte-
> gration into God's order. (Pages 161, 160.)

"But he would steal away to lonely places and pray." Why? Because being alone with God is the secret of being at one with God. You can't be at one with Him, unless you're alone with Him. It was that way with Jesus—it will be that way with the Jesus Generation: Being alone with Him is the secret to their being at one with Him.

So are you alone with Him? Are the silence and solitude of prayer a discipline in your life these days? I know that it's much easier to affirm this discipline than to embrace it!

Anybody who says that getting up early in the morning for solitude and prayer is easy hasn't tried it for very long. But that is precisely the nature of a discipline—you are committed to it, whether it is easy or not! I know it's tough with noisy roommates, I know it's difficult with small children at home, I know it's hard when you come in so late at night and have to leave so early in the morning. And you can be certain that Lucifer will double your trouble when you set out to commit yourself to solitude and prayer, because he, too, knows the truth that being alone with God is the secret to being at one with God.

But do you know any other way to be alone with God than through the discipline of setting aside daily time blocks for that communion? Look again at Jesus' life. You don't think it was easy for Him, do you? As harried and hassled as our contemporary survival is, it's hard to imagine a life more pressed to the limits than the life of Jesus. If anyone could claim periodic exemption from the discipline of prayer on account of busy-ness, couldn't He? Mark describes one of Jesus' weekend schedules:

> That evening, at sundown [Saturday night], they
> brought to him all who were sick or possessed
> with demons. And the whole city was gathered
> around the door. . . . In the morning [Sunday],
> while it was still very dark, he got up and went
> out to a deserted place, and there he prayed.
> (Mark 1:32, 33, 35.)

While the village slumbers, Jesus crawls from between His covers and quietly tiptoes over the sleeping forms of His disciples, as He slips out of the house and up into the hills to be alone with God. We know from the Greek words Mark chose that Jesus awakened during the last watch, which was between 3 and 6 a.m. And the fact that "it was still very dark" indicates that Jesus arose before sunrise, which was usually at 5 a.m. Up till late at night, then up again before the birds at dawn. While that wasn't His daily routine, yet it is true that "often He passed the entire night in prayer and meditation, returning at daybreak to His work among the people" (*The Desire of Ages*, p. 260). Mark's portrayal is clear evidence of the priority that the practice of prayer held in the life of the incarnate God.

Does it necessarily follow that we too should "often" spend entire nights in prayer? No, it does not. Ellen White cautioned against "unbalanced minds that impose upon themselves fasting which the Scriptures do not teach, and prayers and privation of rest and sleep which God has never required" (*Testimonies*, vol. 1, p. 556).

Nevertheless, the example of Jesus remains a clarion summons for the Jesus Generation to the practiced discipline of personal prayer.

For some of us, that quest to be alone with Jesus may, in fact, be met by an occasional arising in the middle of the night—when the house or the trailer or the apartment or the dorm room is hushed in silence. Such an hour may be the most opportune moment for us to be alone with God. What would happen if the next time you unexpectedly awaken in the night or early morning, you considered it an invitation from God to spend some extra, quality time together? That quiet midnight communion can become a hallowed Bethel indeed.

A.G. Sertillanges, in his book *The Intellectual Life*, has the answer:

> Retirement is the laboratory of the spirit; interior solitude and silence are its two wings. All great works are prepared in the desert, including the redemption of the world. The precursors, the followers, the Master Himself, all obeyed or have to obey one and the same law. Prophets, apostles, preachers, martyrs, pioneers of knowledge, inspired artists in every art, ordinary men and the Man-God, all pay tribute to loneliness, to the life of silence, to the night. (Quoted in Willard, p. 101.)

While I was in South Africa in December of 1991, I learned that it really is possible to awaken in the middle of the night for such communion with God. Because of jet lag, I found myself waking up at two in the morning. I would lie there in bed and try all the fall-asleep techniques I could remember. Which only awakened me more! The first time that happened, I was debating whether or not to go ahead and get up and have my usual devotional worship, which for me is the discipline of prayer journaling.* But then the thought struck me, Why get up to read your Bible and write in your journal at all? Why not quietly slip out of bed and kneel in the darkness and simply talk with the God who is certainly awake at this unearthly hour of the night with you?

So it was that I tried doing just that. And I am grateful to testify that I found that night, and continue to find, in Jesus a very present companion in the night watches. How does that classic line go from *The Desire of Ages?* "When every other voice is hushed, and in quietness we wait before Him, the silence of the soul makes more distinct the voice of God" (p. 363).

He is the God who shapes His words for our waiting, listening hearts. But if our worlds are so noisy and busy and frenzied and harried, how will He ever have the chance to commune with us?

Oh, certainly, it won't be the middle of the night for everyone. For others of us it will be the prayer of David, the friend of God, in Psalm 57:8—"I will awake the dawn." And to do that may necessitate thirty minutes earlier to bed so that we can arise thirty minutes earlier the next morning. As someone has wisely said about prayer: "It is not mind over matter; it is mind over mattress." Maybe it's time to abandon Jay Leno late at night so that we can have Jesus Christ early in the morning!

---

*In my book *A New Way to Pray*, I describe in detail that particular method of journaling, and I highly recommend it to all who are seeking a renewed prayer life.

"I will awake the dawn."

"And rising up a great while before day, he got up and went out to a lonely place, and there he prayed." Commenting on that daily reality in Jesus' own hectic survival, *Thoughts from the Mount of Blessing* puts it this way: "Jesus had select places for communion with God, and so should we. We need often to retire to some spot, however humble, where we can be alone with God" (p. 84).

Why did Jesus relentlessly pursue His priority of prayer? Let me conclude with these words from a page in *The Desire of Ages* that is worth photocopying and tucking away in your study and devotional Bible:

> In a life wholly devoted to the good of others, the Saviour found it necessary to withdraw from the thoroughfares of travel and from the throng that followed Him day after day. He must turn aside from a life of ceaseless activity and contact with human needs, to seek retirement and unbroken communion with His Father. As one with us, a sharer in our needs and weaknesses, He was wholly dependent upon God, and in the secret place of prayer He sought divine strength, that He might go forth braced for duty and trial. In a world of sin Jesus endured struggles and torture of soul. In communion with God He could unburden the sorrows that were crushing Him. Here He found comfort and joy.
>
> In Christ the cry of humanity reached the Father of infinite pity. As a man He supplicated the throne of God till His humanity was charged with a heavenly current that should connect humanity with divinity. Through continual communion He received life from God, that He might impart life to the world. *His experience is to be ours.* (Pages 362, 363, emphasis supplied.)

"His experience is to be ours." You see, being alone with

God is the secret to being at one with God. It was that way for Jesus; it must be that way for the Jesus Generation. The results will be unmistakable: "In him [and her] who looks unto the Author and Finisher of our faith the character of Christ will be manifest" (Ibid., p. 280).

On October 12, 1992, NASA scientists decided to commemorate the 500th anniversary of Columbus' landing on the American isles in a very big way! They did it by simultaneously flipping the computer switches on the world's two most powerful radio telescopes, one in California and one in Puerto Rico. These telescopes are so colossal that each dish is a thousand feet wide and 167 feet deep in the center and covers 20 acres! When the scientists flipped both switches, they launched the most ambitious effort humans have ever undertaken to search for communication from extraterrestrial life forms. They want to know if there is intelligent life out there in the far-flung reaches of our universe.

To ascertain the answer, this $100 million, decade-long project will with minute precision analyze all microwave signals that presently beam to our planet around the clock from outer space. There's nothing new about microwave beams; they've been around since the very beginning. What's new is that since October, 1992, scientists are now intentionally scrutinizing these billions and billions of signals through computer analysis. For one reason: they earnestly hope that somehow, someday there will come a radio message beamed to earth from an intelligent life form somewhere in the vast, uncharted universe!

But you don't need a radio telescope or $100 million to pick up signals from intelligent life in the heavens. All you need is a quiet place and a listening heart. For, "When every other voice is hushed, and in quietness we wait before Him, the silence of the soul makes more distinct the voice of God."

4

"Trick or Treat"

It is a sunny and windswept October 31, the Hallowed Eve—so called because tomorrow, November 1, is All Saints Day. And tomorrow, everyone knows, will be the day that the masses will flock to this university campus, and in particular to this university campus church.

And why will they crowd the campus church tomorrow? Simple. They come for a solitary reason. For on display tomorrow will be one of the most astounding and breathtaking collections of holy relics ever assembled in this land. A jagged thorn from Christ's plaited crown of thorns will be showcased—without doubt the greatest relic in the hallowed collection. But also on display tomorrow will be a dusty piece from the baby Jesus' manger, torn fragments of His diapers, glittering portions of the wise men's gold, a crumbling piece of the ascension rock, and a faded strand of Mother Mary's hair.

And why will the visiting crowds pay dearly to view these relics? Ah, because of the decretal that offers every subscribing viewer the promise of a plenary indulgence of two million years. Two million years to be cut off of their temporal punishment in purgatory for this pay-per-view act of worship!

But that is all tomorrow. Which is why today, October 31, 1517, two young men hastily stride across the university campus at Wittenberg. It is a chilly autumn noon. An Augustinian monk and professor named Martin Luther and his assistant, Johanan Schneider, briskly step from the Black Cloister of their order on campus and hurry to the university bulletin board, which doubles as the castle church's door. And there the young German monk affixes to the church entry a list, in Latin, of 95 carefully framed challenges to the Middle Ages' teaching of indulgences.

Unknown to him, this 34-year-old university professor and pastor was igniting a conflagration more fiery than any Hallowed Eve has ever seen since. The mighty blaze of the Protestant Reformation was about to explode!

But nearly five centuries later, where is that fire, where is that flame any more? Where has it gone, the great and holy inferno that once upon a time ignited an entire generation into spiritual fervor? And what shall we answer, we who are the spiritual progeny of the long-forgotten reformers, we who too easily are content with the waning glow that pathetically flickers from the Reformation's dying embers?

Where is that holy fire in the young any more? A graduate student from Poland came up to me after one of our Wednesday evening LifeLine services (the midweek worship service in the university church I pastor). In the course of our visit he reminded me that many of the great revivals in the history of the Christian church began on university campuses: John Wyclif at Oxford University; John Hus at the University of Prague; Martin Luther at the University of Wittenberg; John Wesley also at Oxford University. And the list goes on. University campuses that became the sites of mighty outpourings of God's Spirit upon seeking, searching hearts.

Why at colleges and universities? I wondered. But then it occurred to me that campuses are blessed with the idealism of students—young minds not easily intimidated by stale traditions and cautious adults. Campuses offer a climate of inquiry and discovery. And inherent in that climate is a resident dissatisfaction with the status quo.

You've seen it, too, haven't you? Look into their faces, when the young are gathered to worship, to fellowship, to pray, to study the Holy Scriptures. Gaze for a while into their intensity and earnest expectancy, and you, too, will see and sense an eager seeking after God and His Spirit.

If God is in the habit of igniting church-wide and even world-wide revivals on the campuses of the young, then maybe the Jesus Generation ought to be targeting such flammable tinder for the kingdom of God! Maybe it's time we reignited the embers of revival and reformation. Maybe it's time for a new generation to get serious about the resident secret to such a spiritual conflagration! The very secret that will revive the Jesus Generation in the end.

The question is, Do you know the secret?

Mark did. And in one of his dramatic one-liners, he unabashedly blurts it out at the very beginning of his gospel. Read it for yourself in Mark 1, the very next line after he describes Jesus' baptism: "And the Spirit drove him out into the wilderness" (Mark 1:12). The Greek word for "drove" is *ekballo*, which can be translated to cast out, to drive out, to throw out, to be expelled. It is a very colorful word and is translated throughout the gospels in a myriad of ways. But I like the way the New Revised Standard Version has translated it here: "And the Spirit drove him out."

Without mincing any words, Mark confronts us at the very beginning of the gospel with the secret to Jesus' life: **His was a Spirit-driven life**. "And the Spirit immediately drove Him out into the wilderness."

The fact of life is that we are all driven by something! That old Nissan commercial of a few years ago is still right: "We are driven!" Of course we are. Some of us are driven by the need to be loved and accepted, and we'll do anything to get it and pay any price to have it (which explains some of our behaviors on a date or at a party). We are driven!

Some of us are driven by the need to be acclaimed and applauded, and thus we press our tormented souls on the pathway of ever seeking to be greater and better and smarter and wealthier and holier. We are driven!

But lest someone conclude that it is somehow wrong to be driven, let us affirm those who are moved by the great needs of human suffering and misery and are consequently driven by compassion to make a difference in a dying world. We are all driven.

And so was Jesus. "And the Spirit immediately drove Him out into the wilderness." His was indeed a Spirit-driven life.

Now, if that sounds too militant and too radical, perhaps Luke the beloved physician and historian can temper a bit this portrait of Jesus. Look at his parallel passage: "Jesus, full of the Holy Spirit, returned from the Jordan and was led by the Spirit in the wilderness" (Luke 4:1). Luke's "was led" certainly does temper Mark's "was driven!" Actually, in the original language, Luke's word is correctly translated, "was being led." Which being interpreted means, the Spirit was "in process" with Jesus. That is, Jesus wasn't merely filled with one good dose of the Spirit at His baptism; Luke clearly describes it as a continuing process **after** His baptism. "Jesus, full of the Holy Spirit, . . . was led by the Spirit." The Spirit-driven, Spirit-led life for Jesus kept on happening day after day and night after night.

And by the way, not just for the forty days in the wilderness, either. Luke carefully informs us that after the wilderness experience Jesus was still "in process" with the Holy Spirit, as he indicates later in the same chapter: "Then Jesus, filled with the power of the Spirit, returned to Galilee" (Luke 4:14). Further on in the same chapter Luke quotes Jesus' hometown inaugural sermon—a sermon that declares Jesus is still in process with the Holy Spirit: "The

Spirit of the Lord is upon me, because he has anointed me to bring good news to the poor" (Luke 4:18).

For Jesus, the Spirit-driven life was a daily-driven experience. So it makes all the sense in the world for this line to appear in *Christ's Object Lessons*: "From hours spent with God [Jesus] came forth morning by morning, to bring the light of heaven to men. Daily He received a fresh baptism of the Holy Spirit" (p. 139).

Did you catch that? "Daily He received a fresh baptism of the Holy Spirit." The Spirit-driven, Spirit-led, Spirit-filled life was the **daily** quest and experience of Jesus.

No wonder Jesus spent so much time teaching about the Holy Spirit!

> Christ, the Great Teacher, had an infinite variety of subjects from which to choose, but the one upon which He dwelt most largely was the endowment of the Holy Spirit. What great things He predicted for the church because of this endowment. Yet what subject is less dwelt upon now? What promise is less fulfilled? (*Selected Messages*, book 1, p. 156.)

And what is this promise that we have left so unfulfilled for so long? Without doubt Luke records the greatest promise of the Holy Spirit found in all of sacred Scripture. It is wrapped up in a single line not captured by any other gospel writer. And it comes at the end of a pithy parable. The time has come for the promise, has it not?

> And he said to them, "Suppose one of you has a friend, and you go to him at midnight and say to him, 'Friend, lend me three loaves of bread; for a friend of mine has arrived, and I have nothing to set before him.' And he answers from within, 'Do not bother me; the door has already been locked, and my children are with me in bed; I cannot get up and give you anything.' I tell you, even though

> he will not get up and give him anything because
> he is his friend, at least because of his persistence
> he will get up and give him whatever he needs.
>
> "So I say to you, Ask, and it will be given you;
> search, and you will find; knock, and the door
> will be opened for you. For everyone who asks re-
> ceives, and everyone who searches finds, and for
> everyone who knocks, the door will be opened. Is
> there anyone among you who, if your child asks
> for a fish, will give a snake instead of a fish? Or if
> the child asks for an egg, will give a scorpion?"
> (Luke 11:9-12.)

Look, Jesus says, you want to talk about trick or treating? How many of you, Jesus asks, when the children come to your house on Halloween all dressed up in their very worst . . . how many of you, He wonders, when these tiny little wondrously weird creatures obviously from another terrestrial ball come to ring your doorbell over and over and over again because they don't know that just touching it once will set your pretty little chimes to ringing . . . how many of you, Jesus questions, when you look into those smudge-painted and crooked-masked faces and hear their toothless grins lisp that squeaky "Twick or Tweat" . . . how many of you, Jesus quizzes, will lace your cookies with arsenic and booby trap your apples with razor blades to give to these young ones who have come for their much-anticipated sweet treats? Never mind that you've carefully researched all the historical shadows to Halloween and have theologically concluded that it is woven with pagan superstitions. How many of you, Jesus wonders aloud, would poison your gifts to the children?

Isn't it true that no matter how much you harumph around the house that evening about Halloween being a dentist-sponsored rip-off of the American public, those little children (and I've found that they're getting bigger and more intimidating every new Halloween) will steal your heart? And in spite of your convictions about the origins of this children's holiday, will you not cheerfully and kindly place your *sugarless* treats (and maybe even some *Our Little Friend* and *Primary Treasure* and *Guide* magazines from the church) in their uplifted candy bags? Now, won't you?

Which is precisely Jesus' point in verse 13! "If you then, who are evil, know how to give good gifts to your children, how much more will the heavenly Father give the Holy Spirit to those who ask him!" And in this single promise is found the great secret to the Jesus Generation.

The question is, Do you believe the promise? Is your immediate response to this query, "Why, of course I do! After all, Jesus said it—I believe it"?

If so, then may I ask you why it is that you and I spend so little time asking for the fulfillment of this promise? I hear a lot of prayers; I pray a lot of prayers. But how often around the little worlds where you and I live and move do you hear daily, earnest prayers for the Holy Spirit?

These words are sadly true, are they not?

> The lapse of time has wrought no change in Christ's parting promise to send the Holy Spirit as His representative. It is not because of any restriction on the part of God that the riches of His grace do not flow earthward to men [and women]. If the fulfillment of the promise is not seen as it might be, it is because the promise is not appreciated as it should be. . . . Wherever the need of the Holy Spirit is a matter little thought of, there is seen spiritual drought, spiritual darkness, spiritual declension and death. Whenever minor matters occupy the attention, the divine power which is necessary for the growth and prosperity of the church, and which would bring all other blessings in its train, is lacking, though offered in infinite plentitude. (*The Acts of the Apostles*, p. 50.)

Could that be it? Have we become so preoccupied with

our earthbound trivialities that the fiery promise of the Holy Spirit has long ago slipped our minds and eluded our prayers? Or is it that we have constructed such an immensely complicated theology of the Holy Spirit (pneumatology, as the theologians would say) that nobody is quite sure anymore just how to go about "getting filled up" with what Jesus promised?

That we would be somewhat intimidated and overwhelmed with the very thought of revival and reformation shouldn't be too surprising, considering the preponderance of no doubt worthy books and seminars and tapes and videos and other such marketed tools that all promise us the fulfillment of the promise (if we'll just read and watch and register and send off for and . . . et cetera).

See the ellipses in the quotation on the previous page from *The Acts of the Apostles*? One little sentence was omitted from that paragraph, so it could be emphasized at this point. A single, solitary sentence that eloquently declares the utter simplicity and reliability of Jesus' Luke 11:13 promise of the Holy Spirit. The sentence? "If all were willing, all would be filled with the Spirit."

Nobody needs a doctorate in pneumatology! All you need is a longing heart. The quiet promise is a commanding offer: Just ask your Father in heaven, and He will give you the Holy Spirit. Could it be more simple? *Ask.*

But maybe we aren't aware of the incredible offer Jesus has wrapped up in this promised gift of the Spirit. I wonder if we really are cognizant of the fact that when we claim this *promise* of the Spirit *for* our lives, we are in essence asking for the very *presence* of Jesus *in* our lives. Ponder these words from *The Desire of Ages* for a moment:

> The Holy Spirit is Christ's representative, but divested of the personality of humanity, and independent thereof. Cumbered with humanity, Christ could not be in every place personally. Therefore it was for [our] interest that He should go to the

Father, and send the Spirit to be His successor on earth. . . . By the Spirit the Saviour would be accessible to all. In this sense He would be nearer to [us] than if He had not ascended on high. (Page 669.)

Did you catch that? Jesus is actually nearer to us through the Holy Spirit than if He were physically present on earth right now! You can't get any closer to Jesus than through the Spirit of Jesus. He is Christ's very present, very personal representative to you, and you alone!

Why, it's as if President Clinton calls you this morning from the White House and announces to you that he has already dispatched to you his personal envoy. You can't believe your ears! The president's personal envoy is on Air Force One right now and will be at my door any minute? "I'd come myself," the president continues to speak into your flabbergasted ears, "but I need to stay here in the capital to run the nation. Instead, I'm sending my closest confidant, who knows me better than anyone else in my government."

You collapse in a chair there beside your kitchen phone. But the president goes on. "Anything you need of me, my envoy will be there to provide for you—whatever you've been asking for lately, whatever you've been seeking for in your life, whatever doors you've been knocking on or dreams you've been pursuing. All you have to do is ask," President Clinton assures you. "After all, he's a friend of mine. And I know it won't be long until he's a close friend of yours, too." And with a cheery good-bye, the president hangs up. And you faint.

"If you then, who are evil, know how to give good gifts to your children, how much more will the heavenly Father give the Holy Spirit to those who ask Him!" A gift even the president can't match! *The Desire of Ages* describes the sweeping expanse of this single promise: "This promised blessing, claimed by faith, brings all other blessings in its train" (p. 672). When you get this gift, you've got it all! Because you have Jesus. It is through the Spirit of Jesus that the character of Jesus is emblazoned upon the Jesus Generation. "Christ has given His Spirit as a divine power . . . to impress His own character upon His church" (Ibid. p. 671).

Want to be like Jesus? Than ask for the Spirit of Jesus. "The Holy Spirit is the breath of spiritual life in the soul. *The impartation of the Spirit is the impartation of the life of Christ.* It imbues the receiver with the attributes of Christ" (Ibid., p. 805, emphasis supplied).

There it is, plain and simple. The sure-fire way to become like Jesus is to be filled with Jesus . . . through the Spirit. "Never will the human heart know happiness until it is submitted to be molded by the Spirit of God. *The Spirit conforms the renewed soul to the model, Jesus Christ"* (*Sons and Daughters of God,* p. 282, emphasis supplied). To be like Jesus, become filled with Jesus. Plain. Simple.

But there is one hitch. And it bears repeating—you must *ask.* God will never force His gift on you. The only way you can receive it is to ask for it. I know it isn't how you were brought up by your parents. As a child, it may have been drilled into your thinking that gifts aren't supposed to be asked for; they're to be patiently waited for or hoped for; but never asked for.

Jesus tosses that Gloria Vanderbilt bit of etiquette out the window. Knock on the door for this gift, Jesus invites us. The greatest gift of all won't be pushed or coerced into anybody's life. Our heavenly Father eagerly waits to bequeath the Holy Spirit to His children who ask for it. But the simple secret is in the asking.

As if there were some virtue in asking! Well, there is. Read on:

> God does not say, Ask once, and you shall re-
> ceive. He bids us ask. Unwearyingly persist in
> prayer. The persistent asking brings the petitioner

into a more earnest attitude, and gives him an increased desire to receive the things for which he asks. . . . *The more earnestly and steadfastly we ask, the closer will be our spiritual union with Christ."* (*Christ's Object Lessons,* pp. 145, 146, emphasis supplied.)

No wonder the Jesus Generation asks like Jesus! For the more they ask, the closer they grow to Him. Isn't that incredible? But it's true—the more we ask, the closer we grow to Him. More and more of the Spirit; closer and closer to the Savior.

No wonder Ellen White continues:

Plead for the Holy Spirit. God stands back of every promise He has made. With your Bible in your hands say, I have done as Thou hast said. I present Thy promise, 'Ask, and it shall be given you.' (*Christ's Object Lessons,* p. 147.)

The more we ask, the closer we grow to Him! So ask and ask and ask.

We are not willing enough to trouble the Lord with our petitions, and to ask Him for the gift of the Holy Spirit. The Lord wants us to trouble Him in this matter. He wants us to press our petitions to the throne. (*Fundamentals of Christian Education,* p. 537.)

The more we ask, the closer we grow to Him. No wonder that over and over again, Jesus urges us to ask over and over again.

Then what are we waiting for? Christmas? Why, it will be the greatest Christmas present of all—the Bethlehem of the Holy Spirit, as some have called Pentecost! Christmas, indeed! The incarnation of the Spirit of Jesus in the lives of the Jesus Generation. And all of it and all of Him for the asking!

Then why is it we don't ask any more than we do?

> Since this is the means by which we are to receive
> power, why do we not hunger and thirst for the
> gift of the Spirit? Why do we not talk of it, pray
> for it, and preach concerning it? The Lord is more
> willing to give the Holy Spirit to those who serve
> Him than parents are to give good gifts to their
> children. For the daily baptism of the Spirit every
> worker [and to be a follower of Jesus is to be a
> worker for Jesus] should offer his petition to God.
> (*The Acts of the Apostles*, p. 50.)

Look at how serious the early church was about this promised gift of Jesus! Read the book of Acts in a single sitting, and let your heart become amazed all over again (or as the Kellogg's Corn Flakes commercial puts it: "Taste them again for the first time!") as you gaze upon the utter centrality of the early Christians' companionship with the Holy Spirit. Chapter after chapter after chapter in Acts recount the tales of men and women whose fire for Jesus came from their filling of His Spirit. If it was that way for the church in the beginning, shall it not be that way, too, for the church at the end?

> Shall we be less earnest than were the apostles?
> Shall we not by living faith claim the promises
> that moved them to the depths of their being to
> call upon the Lord Jesus for the fulfillment of
> His word: "Ask, and ye shall receive"? John
> 16:24. Is not the Spirit of God to come to-day in
> answer to earnest, persevering prayer, and fill
> men [and women] with power? . . . Why, then is
> the church so weak and spiritless? (*Testimonies*,
> vol. 7, p. 32.)

It makes you wonder, doesn't it, what it will take for the Jesus Generation to get serious one last time regarding this stupendous promise? How long shall we be content with our fading and waning embers, when God offers a glorious and blazing fire in the end and for the end?

You must know that not all *are* content today. For that reason a growing chain of men and women and young adults around this globe are arising at 6:15 a.m. in their own time zones and are earnestly claiming the promise of Luke 11:13. Because they aren't content for their church to remain "so weak and spiritless," they have covenanted with God, and in effect with each other— though they have never met one another—that they will claim this promise of Jesus every single day that remains until it is fulfilled.

Yes, they seek the personal and daily filling that Jesus promised. But in a unique and united way they have joined together in quest of the mighty apocalyptic fire-fall of Revelation 18 that is to cascade from heaven just before the return of Jesus! Call it the latter rain, if you want to. Or revival and reformation. The nomenclature isn't important now. What matters is that these women and men, young and aged, of the Jesus Generation behold in the rapid disintegration and dysfunction of this planet the sure evidence of the final showdown.

Weighed with a burden to reach this dying race one last time for Jesus, they pour out their hearts to Christ morning after morning. For if Jesus' gift of the Holy Spirit could transform 120 men and women in Jerusalem's upper room long ago—and through them turn the world upside down— think of what His outpouring could do today!

So it is that alone in their prayer closets at 6:15 a.m. (or fifteen minutes past the hour of their awakening)—and together in small prayer groups in offices and schools and factories and neighborhoods and churches and Sabbath Schools—the Jesus Generation is arising to its apocalyptic destiny. They know that the shining hour of fulfillment has come at last. In anticipation and expectation, the Jesus Generation is at last found upon its knees.

"A chain of earnest, praying believers should encircle

the world . . . . to pray for the Holy Spirit." (*Review and Herald*, January 3, 1907.)

> Let us, with contrite hearts, pray most earnestly that now, in the time of the latter rain, the showers of grace may fall upon us. . . . If we pray for the blessing in faith, we shall receive it as God has promised. (*Testimonies to Ministers*, p. 509.)

> The descent of the Holy Spirit upon the church is looked forward to as in the future; but it is the privilege of the church to have it now. Seek for it, pray for it, believe for it. We must have it, and Heaven is waiting to bestow it. (*Review and Herald*, March 19, 1895.)

"We must have it" indeed! Hasn't the hour come for us to link hands and hearts around our neighborhoods and parishes and across our cities and nations in a chain of impassioned seekers? Yes, you can begin tomorrow morning in your own prayer closet or corner. But why not get on the telephone and share this quest with a few of your friends and family? Why not form a small prayer and study group that can become an ignited catalyst for a renewed mission to reach your own neighborhood or campus or office? God knows how desperately our planet and our church need the fire of the Spirit. "And Heaven is waiting to bestow it."

Plainly and simply, the time has come to ask.

I couldn't believe my ears! But there it was coming over the public address system of the Baltimore-Washington International Airport. It was the most peculiar announcement I've heard in an airport. So much so that I hurriedly grabbed a piece of paper and scribbled it down.

As I was waiting at the gate for my own flight home, I heard a voice come over the intercom at the gate across the concourse hallway: "For those of you waiting here at gate 9 for flight #123, your plane is now ready for departure.

Our flight attendants are here and ready to service your boarding. However," and here's what was so startling, "we have yet to locate a front-end crew. We are trying to find one here in the airport. As soon as we have a front-end crew, we will be ready to depart."

Can you believe it! They have a plane and a lot of flight attendants and a gate full of passengers; but they're missing one small but significant detail—they don't have a front-end crew! Which being interpreted means, they haven't found a pilot and navigator yet!

Boy, was I glad I wasn't booked for that flight! No telling whom they finally found to fly their plane!

No front-end crew. The fact of the matter is that the Jesus Generation cannot afford to travel without a front-end crew, either. We have the promise—the divine Pilot and Navigator are ready. But they will not board our flight unless they are asked. Isn't it high time that the Jesus Generation ask them?

> Could there be a convocation of all the churches
> of earth, the object of their united cry should be
> for the Holy Spirit. When we have that, Christ our
> sufficiency is ever present. We shall have every
> want supplied. We shall have the mind of Christ.
> (Ellen White, *Manuscript Releases*, vol. 2, p. 24.)

At 6:15 a.m. tomorrow, won't you join me in asking?

"If you then, who are evil, know how to give good gifts to your children, how much more will the heavenly Father give the Holy Spirit to those who ask him"!

5

"R.I.P."

It was Will Rogers, the cowboy philosopher and humorist, who once said, "If 10 percent of campaign promises were kept, there would be no inducement to go to heaven." He's probably right! Because if all the political promises made during the last presidential campaign in fact came true, we'd have heaven on earth! Almost. No poverty, no deficit, no illiteracy, with health care for all, world peace, and on and on. Promises, promises, promises. Which is why we all have such a hard time trusting politicians and their promises anymore.

The Gallup organization surveyed the nation to ascertain what professions we trust most and least. Which profession do you suppose the public considers the most trusted, most ethical and honest of professions? Do you want to guess? The answer may surprise you—it's pharmacists and druggists. Americans trust the people selling pills more than any other profession. Which is a well-deserved feather in the caps, or at least on the prescription labels, of our pharmacists, to be sure.

But after pharmacists, it's all downhill! And unfortunately that includes your profession and mine. I was tempted to replicate the entire list that Gallup compiled, but realizing that we're all there somewhere between the top and the bottom, I decided it to be the better part of pastoral prudence to omit it. In fact, I'm not even going to quote Gallup as to who's at the bottom of the trust list of professions. And really, I don't have to, since everybody already knows about the proverbial . . . Oh well, you guessed it anyway.

But I don't suppose you're surprised to learn that not far from the bottom are politicians. Which is why trust has been such a big deal in the recent national campaigns. Not that it's made much difference in the end. But it certainly makes the headlines.

It makes you wonder how God would fare in an election today. If God were put on a ballot, how would He come out? Does He rank very high on our country's trust list? Would you find the Father up there with the pharmacists, or down there with the politicians? Is there anybody left who still trusts Him? Why, even Jesus Himself wondered aloud, "When the Son of Man comes, will he find faith on earth?" (Luke 18:8). Faith . . . trust. I wonder how God would've rated in the voting booth.

The dictionary defines *trust* as: a confident reliance on the integrity, honesty, veracity, or justice of another; to rely upon another; to commit to the care of another; to believe in another; to allow another to do something without the fear of consequences.

That's the tough part, isn't it? To allow someone to do something to you without the fear of consequences. Which is why we teach our children not to trust strangers. Because if you don't know someone, then you have absolutely no idea whether he or she will honor your trust or betray it. So most of us live by the adage: You can't trust someone you don't know.

Afraid to trust strangers—afraid to trust politicians. But

what about God? Oh, sure, the pennies in our pockets jingle, "In God We Trust." You can't miss the national motto on our coinage. But is it your personal motto, too? Do we really trust God? And if we're saying "yes," then why is it we worry so much? And why are we so afraid so often?

Whenever I gaze into that sleeping face drenched with the spray of the furious storm—that face that keeps rolling and pitching from side to side and yet keeps on sleeping—I exclaim to myself, That has to be trust! How else can you explain His lying there so serenely, so peacefully, so sleepfully in that sea-sickening, storm-blasted fishing skiff? If that isn't trust, I don't know what is.

I know how I feel when the plane I'm flying on hits one of those famous CATs (pockets of "clear air turbulence") and suddenly pitches up, drops down, or jerks sideways. With me, it's all instinctive. I may be in the middle of a conversation with my seatmate, but in that jolt of turbulence, you'll find me reflexively grabbing onto my armrest in a millisecond! I do try hard not to embarrass myself in mid-sentence. But if the choice is between embarrassment or security, my white-knuckled grip on the armrest declares that I'll take hanging on over looking tough any day!

But there is Jesus, sound asleep in a boat that appears headed straight down to Davy Jones' locker. Soak in Mark's full-sensory account of that moment:

> On that day, when evening had come, he said to them, "Let us go across to the other side." And leaving the crowd behind, they took him with them in the boat, just as he was. Other boats were with him. A great windstorm arose, and the waves beat into the boat, so that the boat was already being swamped. But he was in the stern, asleep on the cushion. (Mark 4:35-38.)

Here they are peacefully sailing under the tranquil evening canopy of stars over Galilee, when one of those infamous killer winds comes raging out of the mountain gorges to the east! And in a crashing moment of pitch-black fury, the night sky rages into a panoply of destruction. There in the midnight pall, the disciples' puny dingy begins to pitch and toss like abandoned flotsam on the towering waves. Four-foot . . . six-foot . . . eight-foot waves thunder and crash into that little skiff in the awful darkness.

You can't possibly bail this baby out fast enough! The ship is going down. Fast. And the look of panic on Peter's ashen face announces their doom to the entire boat-load. "Prepare to meet thy God!"

And then in a split second of white thunder and lightning, they spot the Man they'd forgotten all about, asleep in the stern of their drowning vessel. Above the shriek of the gale, their desperate cries wail, "Teacher, do you not care that we are perishing?" (verse 38).

Jesus' peaceful repose is broken. His tired eyes blink as He awakens to the midnight fury. Not a trace of fear on that arising face. Bracing Himself between the gunwales, the Master stands amid the heaving crew.

> He woke up and rebuked the wind, and said to the sea, "Peace! Be still!" Then the wind ceased, and there was a dead calm. He said to them, "Why are you afraid? Have you still no faith?" And they were filled with great awe and said to one another, "Who then is this, that even the wind and the sea obey him?" (Mark 4:39-41.)

Let me ask you a question: What is the opposite of fear? Easy answer, you say—peace. But as my children exclaim, *Not!* Jesus' words to those dripping and shivering disciples contain the answer, "Why are you afraid? Have you still no faith?" (Verse 40.) The opposite of fear is faith and trust.

Remember our dictionary definition for trust? "To allow another to do something to you without fear of the consequences." Trust is the opposite of fear. That was why Jesus could sleep so soundly and peacefully through that tempest.

Oswald Chambers, in his classic, *My Utmost for His*

Highest, defines faith and trust in this way: "Faith is unutterable trust in God, trust which never dreams that He will not stand by us" (p. 242). It never even crossed the mind of Jesus that God wouldn't stand beside Him. So with unutterable trust, He falls sound asleep in the midst of a storm! When your life is in God's hands, His peace is in your heart.

And to all those might think, "Oh, sure, if I were the incarnate God, I wouldn't be afraid either, since I would know that I was God and nothing could harm me." Wrong again!

> When Jesus was awakened to meet the storm, He was in perfect peace. There was no trace of fear in word or look, for no fear was in His heart. But He rested not in the possession of almighty power. It was not as the 'Master of earth and sea and sky' that He reposed in quiet. That power He had laid down, . . . He trusted in the Father's might. It was in faith—faith in God's love and care—that Jesus rested. (*The Desire of Ages,* p. 336.)

Trusting His Father, He slept through the storm. Jesus' gentle chiding of His disciples is proof enough that His restful trust can be ours, too.

> As Jesus rested by faith in the Father's care, so we are to rest in the care of our Saviour. If the disciples had trusted in Him, they would have been kept in peace. . . . Whether on the land or on the sea, if we have the Saviour in our hearts, there is no need to fear. Living faith in the Redeemer will smooth the sea of life, and will deliver us from danger in the way that He knows best. (Ibid., emphasis supplied.)

Did you catch that? "If we have the Saviour in our hearts, there is no need to fear." Why should we fear? Hasn't Jesus shown Himself to be the Master of any crisis and of every storm?

I don't know what kind of storm is pounding your little skiff these days. Your boat may have been beaten and battered lately by the pounding tempest of temptations. You may already be bailing your life out as fast as you can, but your ship is still going down. And there seems to be no way out of the sin that howls like a midnight gale through your heart. You may be struggling hard against the raging winds of guilt and failure. The thunder of your own tormented conscience has blown a maelstrom into your life. Nobody sails smoothly through life. We've all got our tempests.

But the Good News is that there still is Somebody who can stand up in our sinking skiffs and command the storm to cease and desist. The perennial challenge for us is to remember He's in the boat! And remembering, to turn the ropes and rudder over to Him. That's what trust is all about. Because when your life is in God's hands, then His peace is in your heart. Just look at Jesus! His secret was His trust.

You may roam wherever you wish throughout the gospel stories, but you will always run into Jesus quietly trusting His Father.

How else can you explain the very next story in the synoptics of the madmen who come screaming down from the pock-marked lakeside cliffs early the next dawn? After their near miss with death, the disciples' knees are still weak as they clamor over the gunwales of their beached vessel. The morning chill is crisp and invigorating. They yawn and stretch their water-logged forms there on the sand. And then they freeze! The blood-curdling shrieks of the two demoniacs rend the dawn's tranquility. Broken chains and bloody torsos and foaming mouths—the madmen tear straight toward the small band of hapless arrivals.

Twelve grown men are frozen in their sandy tracks for one split second. And then with screeching tires and burning rubber, the Twelve throw themselves into reverse and streak back to the skiff. Peter, with an adrenalin shove, launches the boat onto the placid lake waters. Gulping in the tranquil air, the Twelve quickly count noses to make certain all are safe. But number thirteen, where is He?

The men whirl around in the boat and gasp. He's where they left Him. Jesus stands there unflinching and unafraid, His penetrating eyes fixed on the two clawing demoniacs who wildly careen toward this intruder. But even in the presence of Lucifer's fury, Jesus is unshaken. He quietly goes on trusting His Father. No trace of fear on His countenance. Because when your life is in God's hands, His peace is in your heart. Even when all hell breaks loose.

The life of Jesus is living proof that trusting God is the secret to lasting peace.

There they are, expectorating in Jesus' face on the eve of His execution. Their spittle clings to His beard. His back has been shredded open into a mass of bloody wounds by the Roman flagrum, or whip. A twisted crown of jagged thorns plaited and pressed onto His brow, Jesus can stand there without a word of retaliation, without a curse of retribution. He keeps trusting His Father. And He goes on proving it true that when your life is in God's hands, His peace is in your heart.

Even in death, mind you! Death on a scarlet cross.

It was now about noon, and darkness came over the whole land until three in the afternoon, while the sun's light failed; and the curtain of the temple was torn in two. Then Jesus, crying with a loud voice, said, "Father, into your hands I commend my spirit." Having said this, he breathed his last. (Luke 23:44-46.)

And what did that loud voice (Greek: *mega phone*, from whence comes our word *megaphone*) cry? "I commend my spirit into your hands, Father!" The Greek word for "commend" here is also translated "entrust" in Luke 12:48. So Jesus' death cry can just as accurately be read, "I entrust my spirit into your hands, Father." Trust in the face of death! Calvary's lonely cross is an eternal testimony to such conquering trust!

I don't want to sound morbid, but if I am able to choose the last words I speak before I die, let the record show that I would like to die with these words of absolute trust on my lips. The first Christian martyr did a few chapters later in Acts 7. Stephen died uttering the words—"Lord Jesus, receive my spirit." He died the way Jesus died. And Jesus died the way He lived—trusting His life into His Father's hands.

But Stephen isn't the only one who died like Jesus. So did John Hus, the Bohemian pastor and reformer, who died tethered to the stake. His last words were: "I do commit my spirit into Thy hands, O Lord Jesus, for Thou has redeemed me." (And then, as they lighted his pyre, he began to sing!) These were also Bernard's last words, and Luther's, and Melancthon's. And if the truth could be known, how many have died upon this earth with the last words of Jesus upon their lips?

And what was true for generations past must become true for the Jesus Generation. The **last words** of Christ must become the **life words** of the Jesus Generation—that generation of men and women and young adults and children who will be living at the end of time. They will know well the last words of Jesus. For His last words will have become their life words.

How do I know? Because of how the Apocalypse describes this end-time generation! Read again the familiar portrayal of God's final community of faith in Revelation 14:12. Here are they "who hold fast to the faith of Jesus." How did Oswald Chambers put it earlier? "Faith is unutterable trust in God, trust which never dreams that He will not stand by us."

Father, into your hands I entrust my spirit, my soul, my life, my all. It's all Yours, Jesus; I'm all Yours. And I'm not afraid of the consequences, because I trust You. If You want to send me through the middle of a storm, I'll trust You. If

I can honor You at the top of a cross, I'll trust You. So prays the Jesus Generation.

A friend of mine, Joe Engelkemier, taught me the most radical prayer I've ever heard. And I am only now learning to pray it. I had never heard of this prayer before, and perhaps you haven't either. But without question it represents the deepest level of trust a human can have in God. The prayer goes like this: Lord, do whatever You want, do whatever it takes—my life is in Your hands.

It is the prayer of the cross, is it not? "Father, into Your hands I entrust my spirit. Do whatever You want, do whatever it takes—my life is in Your hands." Why, it's the prayer of the garden, too! Remember Jesus' great convulsing sobs in Gethsemane? "Father, if you are willing, remove this cup from me; yet not my will, but yours be done" (Luke 22:42). Which being interpreted means, "Father, do whatever You want, do whatever it takes—my life is in Your hands."

The great prayer of radical trust. The question is, How? How can such trust become mine? The secret is found in the very psalm Jesus was quoting as He hung on the cross: "Into your hand I commit my spirit; you have redeemed me, O Lord, faithful God" (Psalm 31:5). But read on through the rest of the psalm.

> *But I trust in you, O Lord;*
> *I say, "You are my God."*
> *My times are in your hand;*
> *deliver me from the hand of*
> *my enemies and persecutors.*
> *Let your face shine upon your*
> *servant;*
> *save me in your steadfast*
> *love. (Verses 14-16.)*

Then the secret of David's trust in God is revealed in his closing line: "Be strong, and let your heart take courage, all you who wait for the Lord" (verse 24).

Though your life may be in shambles right now (as Jesus' life was on the cross), God has not forgotten you. All hell was in celebration that Friday when Jesus breathed out His last! Little did Lucifer and his demons realize that in less than 48 hours, the most stupendous miracle of all time would shatter their history and ours forever. And at Sunday's dawning, there shone the irrefutable truth that you can trust the God who will have the last word. No matter what's going on or what's shaking down in your life right now, you can trust the God who promises to have the last word! "Be strong, and let your heart take courage, all you who wait for the Lord."

Robert Browning was right when he wrote in his poem, "Rabbi Ben Ezra":

> *Our times are in His hand*
> *Who saith "A whole I planned,*
> *Youth shows but half; trust God:*
> *see all, nor be afraid!"*

"Trust God; see all, nor be afraid." Look at who is on your side!

> They [the Jesus Generation] are to contend with supernatural forces, but they are assured of supernatural help. All the intelligences of heaven are in this army. And more than angels are in the ranks. The Holy Spirit, the representative of the Captain of the Lord's host, comes down to direct the battle. . . . The power of Omnipotence is enlisted in behalf of those who trust in God. (*The Desire of Ages*, p. 352.)

No wonder the **last words** of Jesus are the **life words** of the Jesus Generation. "Do whatever You want, do whatever it takes—my life is in Your hands." There can be no deeper level of trust than to pray and mean that prayer. Radical trust in God. No matter what the price—no matter what the consequences.

As Revelation describes this end-time generation, "They did not cling to life even in the face of death." Like Job, they cry out, "Though he slays me, yet will I trust him." Nobody said the final showdown would be a piece of cake; but there will be peace of mind and heart. Because when your life is in God's hands, His peace is in your heart.

Brennan Manning, in *The Lion and the Lamb*, tells the story of an elderly man who lay dying. When the priest came to anoint him, he noticed an empty chair by the bed and asked who had just been visiting. The sick man replied, "I place Jesus on that chair and I talk to Him." He went on to explain how years earlier, when he'd been finding it difficult to pray, a friend had told him that praying to Jesus was like talking with a friend and suggested that he imagine Jesus sitting in a chair where he could speak with Him and listen to what He said in reply. "I've had no trouble praying ever since."

Some days later, the daughter of this man came to the priest to inform him that her father had just died. She explained, "Because he seemed so content, I left him alone for a couple of hours. When I got back, I noticed a strange thing, though—his head was resting not on the bed but on an empty chair that was beside his bed."

"Then Jesus, crying with a loud voice, said, 'Father, into your hands I commend my spirit.' Having said this, he breathed his last."

R.I.P. Those mossy letters carved upon weather-beaten slabs of granite in abandoned cemeteries are the quiet truth of trust. For the old man on the empty chair and Jesus on the cross were both right: When it comes to living and dying, trust means that you can rest in peace.

6

Lexus and the
Last Temptation

The solitary figure moves into the blinding light of the desert sun. Stretched before him beneath the withering blaze is a vast expanse of cracked and wrinkled earth. Brown and barren, it offers for his solace not a single tree or a solitary blade. In the distance, the bald, rust-tone mountains lie atop the horizon like a row of rusty skull pans.

The lone figure trudges on, his lips cracked and parched, his eyes tired and strained, his face burned by the sun and beaten by the wind—a wind that still bites at his ankles with the stinging sand from the desert floor. But there is nothing to slake his dusty thirst here; there is nothing to feed his gnawing hunger. The solitary one turns away.

Deliberately, this lone inhabitant of the wild desert picks his way across the burning, rocky floor until he rests at last in the sweltering shade of a barren hillside outcropping. He has been there before to pray. He returns again, now to rest a body that has gone nearly six weeks without food. Forty days ago, the heavens had been rent with a shaft of light and an echo of a Voice that declared the dripping baptismal candidate to be the beloved Son of God. But that was forty days ago. Now the voice of God seems but the mirage of a faraway memory as the solitary Man sweats and suffers alone in the desert fire.

Suddenly another voice breaks the hot and oppressive calm. The Man beneath the outcropping whirls around to face the intruder. What a comedy of contrasts, this portrait of these two beings! One face is emaciated and haggard, with eyes sunken into the hollow skin of intentional foodlessness, and cheekbones protruding in pathetic prominence. It is a face that so often in black and white has stared back at us from behind the barbed wires of other deserts called Buchenwald and Auschwitz and Kampuchea and Sarejevo.

But the other face that desert morning is bathed with an ethereal glow—smooth, clear, noble, and proud—the face of one who pretends to reside in heaven, but who for this showdown has ascended from hell.

Back in 1903 these words were written:

> While in the wilderness, Christ fasted, but He was insensible to hunger. Engaged in constant prayer to His Father for a preparation to resist the adversary, Christ did not feel the pangs of hunger. He spent the time in earnest prayer, shut in with God. It was as if He were in the presence of His Father. . . . and He did not realize any sense of hunger until the forty days of His fast were ended. The vision passed away, and then, with strong craving Christ's human nature called for food. Now was Satan's opportunity to make his assault. He resolved to appear as one of the angels of light that had appeared to Christ in His vision. (*SDA Bible Commentary*, vol. 5, p. 1080.)

Lucifer is the first to speak. Please note that his *modus operandi* hasn't changed over the centuries. He relishes the idea of attacking his victim soon after that individual has made a public commitment for God. Forty days earlier, Jesus was baptized. Now the devil strikes. It is a timely warning for all who have recently and publicly confessed their allegiance to this same Jesus. Be on the watch, "for like a roaring lion your adversary the devil prowls around, looking for someone to devour" (1 Peter 5:8).

It's a masterful strategy Satan has devised in his surprise attack on Jesus: He will pretend to be an angelic ambassador straight from the throne-room of the Father. Ellen White wrote that Lucifer, in fact, claimed to be the very same angel who grabbed the hand of Abraham as he prepared to sacrifice his boy Isaac (Ibid., p. 1081). The insinuation? "This has all been a test, and like Abraham, you have passed it. You need not take one more step down the pathway you've chosen. For the Father accepts your willingness to travel the blood-stained way. And I have been sent to tell you that you won't have to go that way now. As it was with Abraham, so with you—we simply wanted to know if you were willing to follow through. And you were! So here I am to deliver you!"

The shining angel pauses, as if in reflection. "Although, I suppose I should tell you that one of the most powerful angels of heaven has been banished from the courts above . . . and I wonder. You certainly don't *look* like any Son of God. In fact, I'm beginning to think . . . are *you* that fallen angel? Why else would God and man have forsaken you here in this desert?"

But then that angelic face cunningly lights up. "Ah, but if you *are* the Son of God, do you see these stones?" The angel stoops over to pick up a sun-baked rock. "Here. Take this one and turn it into bread. Then it'll be perfectly clear that you *are* the one God sent me to deliver. If you're the Son of God, it should be a piece of cake for you to turn it into cake and eat it."

As long as you and I live, that dare will never, ever be a temptation for us! We could hold a stone in our hands and chant to it till we were blue in the face, and not once would that rock even hint at becoming a loaf of bread or a piece of cake! Why? Because we don't have the wherewithal to perform such a miracle. But the incarnate God did. I remind you that Jesus didn't have the power of God **at** His fingertips; He had that power **in** His fingertips. One word, and He who would call the dead to life could have turned that rock to bread.

But if He had, it would all have been over—curtains, *finis,* the end. And Lucifer would have howled to high heaven: "See, I told you, universe, that human beings never had the capacity to trust and obey God. Why, even the God-Man can't do it, which is proof that I am right and God is wrong!" If Jesus had resorted to His divinity to face off the devil, it would instantly have shattered the plan of salvation by proving Lucifer's point: God is an arbitrary tyrant who demands from His creatures an obedience impossible for them to give Him.

But Jesus recognizes His nemesis in that being of light. The memory of His Father's voice at His baptism still echoes within Him. And staring into those disguised but hellish eyes, Jesus licks His parched and cracked lips and with quiet force responds: "It is written, 'One does not live by bread alone, but by every word that comes from the mouth of God'" (Matthew 4:4).

Round one—down but not out! Lucifer craftily smiles: "You want to play the 'It is written' game? Good! Because I can play it, too. Come with me." And with that, Jesus is whisked by the enemy north and eastward until the two of them are perched upon the towering golden pinnacle of Jerusalem's holy temple.

If, in the majestic temple complex, Satan chose Herod's royal portico that overhangs the Kedron Valley, then the distance from the pinnacle to the valley floor measured 450 feet straight down—and that's equivalent to a forty-five-story building! More than enough height to give somebody like me the willies! I was in Boston a few months ago and rode with a friend up to the observatory atop the John Hancock building. It was all securely glassed in, but never mind! I got jittery just getting close to the glass. Try to imagine yourself perched on a pinnacle dome, without railings, forty-five stories into the sky, and standing beside someone who'd love to push you off!

Now for the "it is written" game. "Look, Jesus, you know the rabbinical tradition that declares that the Messiah will come down out of heaven and reveal Himself on the roof of the holy place of this temple. Well, here's your chance to rally your people."

> If you are the Son of God, throw yourself down;
> for it is written, "He will command his angels con-
> cerning you," and "On their hands they will bear
> you up, so that you will not dash your foot
> against a stone." (Verse 6.)

But let the record show that whenever Satan plays the Bible-quoting game with you, he conveniently omits the reminder that God can keep you faithful in your obedience to Him.

With cunning precision, Satan excises from his quotation of Psalm 91 the words, "to keep you in all your ways." Because it is Lucifer's strategy to thwart any reminder that God is able to protect you in any circumstance, under any temptation!

But Jesus will not be duped. Teetering on that pinnacle and standing next to the one being in the universe who would love to throw Him off, Jesus replies: "Again it is written, 'Do not put the Lord your God to the test'" (verse 7).

Lucifer, in satanic rage, now strips away his disguising mask. No more Mr. Nice Guy now as he towers above Jesus and "avows himself the leader of rebellion and the god of this world" (*The Desire of Ages*, p. 129).

"Alright, if you want to play for keeps, then I'm ready." He plays the last ace in his hand.

> Again, the devil took him to a very high mountain
> and showed him all the kingdoms of the world
> and their splendor; and he said to him, "All these I
> will give you, if you will fall down and worship
> me." (Verses 8, 9.)

"You can have it all," Satan whispers. "I'll give it all to you with no blood, no guts, no cross, no sacrifice, no pain, no loss. I'll give it all back to you—the world and its inhabitants—they're all yours. *If* only you will bow down and worship me. Be reasonable. God's way takes too long. My way will give it to you now. Right now!"

Do you think this final ace in Satan's hand was no temptation for Jesus? The fact that Jesus fell dying to the ground when it was over is proof enough!

With the last ounce of strength and faith left within Him, Jesus whirls full face toward Lucifer. "Jesus said to him, 'Away with you, Satan! for it is written, "Worship the Lord your God, and serve only him"'" (verses 10, 11).

And then with "the pallor of death upon His face," as *The Desire of Ages* describes it, Jesus falls to the earth.

We will never be able fully to fathom the force and fury of the satanic attack on the Savior that wilderness day:

> To keep His glory veiled as the child of a fallen
> race, this was the most severe discipline to which
> the Prince of life could subject Himself. Thus He
> measured His strength with Satan. He who had
> been expelled from heaven fought desperately for
> the mastery over the One of whom in the courts
> above he had been jealous. What a battle was this!
> No language is adequate to describe it. (*SDA Bible
> Commentary*, vol. 5, pp. 1081, 1082.)

This is neither play-acting nor shadow-boxing! This isn't Darth Vader against Luke Skywalker. This is Michael versus the Dragon, Christ against Satan, the incarnate God versus Lucifer. The champions of light and darkness battle face to face in the desert sands for the allegiance and mastery of the human race!

Something deep within tells me that all of us need to bow low in humility before the Jesus of the wilderness battle and confess that we have never taken our own temptations as seriously! How could He so radically and resolutely obey His Father in the face of such a demonic barrage?

You may not like the answer, because it's bluntly simple and just as bluntly plain that it must become our answer, too.

> In the days of his flesh, Jesus offered up prayers and supplications, with loud cries and tears, to the one who was able to save him from death, and he was heard because of his reverent submission. Although he was a Son, he learned obedience through what he suffered. (Hebrews 5:7, 8.)

Plain and simple: The incarnate God of the universe had to learn obedience, because for the human race, obedience isn't something you're born with.

In fact, for us, "obey" is a four-letter word, isn't it? "I don't like anybody telling me what to do," is the obstinate cry of our me-first generation. "Learn obedience? Gimme a break!" So we keep breaking down and giving in, don't we? After all, as Mark Twain said: "I can resist anything except temptation." I mean, what's the big deal? You win a few, you lose a few. It all comes out in the wash. But the question is, Whose wash? And the answer is Lucifer's, of course! And he doesn't get anything very clean!

Listen to Oswald Chambers for a moment in one of the most perceptive definitions of temptation I've ever read:

> Temptation is a suggested shortcut to the realization of the highest at which I aim—not towards what I understand as evil, but towards what I understand as good. (*My Utmost for His Highest*, p. 261.)

Do you know what Chambers is saying? The temptations you and I fall for are often shortcuts to our highest dreams and loftiest goals. That's how it was with the temptation of Jesus: "You don't need the cross—I have a shortcut that will get you where you want to go much more quickly, much more easily, much less painfully. Forget this radical obedience stuff—your Father isn't always right!"

Shortcuts—that's what Satan offers. How often his temptations offer shortcuts to good and lofty goals. Obviously there's nothing wrong with eating, is there? Or drinking? So what if I cope with loneliness and stress by eating? So what if to gain companionship and acceptance, I drink? They're all commendable goals, aren't they? What's a little shortcut now and then?

There's nothing wrong with sexual fulfillment, is there? Didn't God make us sexual creatures? So why get upset about sharing my sexuality on a date or outside of marriage? I need to be loved and needed and fulfilled—so why not? And besides, we aren't all born with the same orientation.

There's nothing wrong or evil with success, is there? So what's to worry about this shortcut power play to get me to the top? A little academic cheating will get me the top grades I've got to have.

There's nothing wrong with making money, is there? So what's the big deal about this little adjustment of the figures on my tax returns or on my time card? Shortcuts—the devil's temptations are shortcuts to some admirable ambition or God-given desire.

Remember, there is no sin in being tempted. The story of Jesus is shining proof of that fact. As Hebrews 4:15 triumphantly declares: He "was in all points tempted like as we are, yet without sin" (KJV). Temptations turn into sins, however, when we become impatient with God's long journey and voluntarily choose the shortcut instead.

If Joseph had taken the shortcut with Potipher's wife, we never would have known his story. If Jesus had taken the shortcut with Lucifer's offer, there would be no story at all! No, the fact is that sin is birthed in the heart when the mind opts out of God's plan and chooses the shortcut instead.

For, you see, in the end temptations are usually a choice between God and sin's shortcut. Listen to Oswald Chambers again: "Sin is red-handed mutiny against God. Either God or sin must die in my life" (Ibid., p. 175). They cannot coexist, for no person can serve two masters. Which is why sin is red-handed mutiny against God. Which is also why radical obedience is best defined as our voluntary choosing of God in the face of a nearly overmastering temptation to reject His way. Radical obedience is to choose as Jesus did.

To sin or not to sin—day in and day out, night after night, that remains our choice. Dallas Willard, in his book *The Spirit of the Disciplines*, is absolutely right:

> If one day I assure my Christian friends that I intend to "quit sinning" and arrive at a stage where I can perfectly follow Jesus Christ, they will most likely be scandalized and threatened—or at least very puzzled. "Who do you think you are?" they would probably say. Or they might think, "What is he really up to?" But if, on the other hand, I state that I do not intend to stop sinning or that I do not plan ever to follow my Lord in actuality, they will be equally upset. And for good reason. How can Jesus be my Lord if I don't even *plan* to obey him? . . . I must do one or the other. Either I must intend to stop sinning or *not* intend to stop. There is no third possibility. I must plan to follow Jesus fully or not plan to follow him. (Pages 12, 13, emphasis his.)

The choice that faces the Jesus Generation today is either the pursuit of sinlessness or the pursuit of sinfulness. "Either I must intend to stop sinning or *not* intend to stop." There is no third possibility, much as you and I might like to craft one to avoid the pitfalls of legalism or perfectionism.

But the fact remains that there are only two choices for all humans: to sin—or not to sin. Or, to frame it in a more positive context, to trust—or not to trust.

Jesus Himself cut straight to the soul of the issue when He declared in the Sermon on the Mount that none of us can serve two masters (see Matthew 6:24). Our choices are not between three masters or four masters. Only two—God or Lucifer. Whom shall we trust? To trust His Father's promises or to yield to Lucifer's promptings—that was the fiery crucible of Jesus' wilderness temptations. And because He learned obedience, He made the right choice—to trust His Father in radical obedience. To trust and obey.

How does that old hymn go? "Trust and obey, for there's no other way, to be happy in Jesus, but to trust and obey." That was our Savior's choice. Then again, you can sing it like the little boy who learned the song at Sabbath School. But when he came home to sing it to his mother, he got the words slightly mixed up as he sang to her: "Trust and OK, for there's no other way." But the boy was right! Because trust and obey means trust and OK—saying OK to God for the long haul. Just like Jesus in the wilderness:

> So [too] we may resist temptation, and force Satan to depart from us. Jesus gained the victory through submission [to obey] and faith in God [to trust], and by the apostle He says to us, "Submit yourselves therefore to God. Resist the devil, and he will flee from you. Draw nigh to God, and He will draw nigh to you." James 4:7, 8. We cannot save ourselves from the tempter's power; he has conquered humanity, and when we try to stand in our own strength, we shall become a prey to his devices; but "the name of the Lord is a strong tower: the righteous runneth into it, and is safe." Prov. 18:10. Satan trembles and flees before the weakest soul who finds refuge in that mighty name. (*The Desire of Ages*, pp. 130, 131.)

What a marvelous promise! The enemy trembles and flees before the weakest of us who cries out the mighty name of Jesus! Do you know what that means? The next time that too-familiar, nearly overpowering temptation comes flooding over you, *you don't have to give in!* Resist. Cry out the name of Jesus. Intensely focus your mind on the pure and noble face of your Lord. See Jesus standing before you in His resplendent armor of glory. Visualize that flaming sword of light in His hand raised in your defense, and cry out to Him: "Lord Jesus, I want to remain true to You and obey You more than anything else, but Satan threatens to overpower me. Save me, Jesus—save me now!"

Nobody—*nobody*—has lost a battle with that name upon his or her lips: Jesus, save me! You may also fall exhausted to the ground, but you will bow down victorious in Christ. For the triumphant name and the enabling power of Jesus will always make possible your radical obedience to God!

Mark well this assurance of deliverance and promise of victory:

> The soul that is yielded to Christ becomes His own fortress, which He holds in a revolted world, and He intends that no authority shall be known in it but His own. *A soul thus kept in possession by the heavenly agencies is impregnable to the assaults of Satan.* (Ibid., p. 324, emphasis supplied.)

An impregnable fortress in Christ—what more can you and I ask for in this twilight hour of human history? No wonder the wise man exclaimed, "The name of the Lord is a strong tower; the righteous run into it and are safe" (Proverbs 18:10). In a blending of metaphors, the ringing assurance is that in a daily friendship with Christ our lives can find a strong tower of defense against the enemy, for with Jesus we shall be impregnable fortresses which He holds amidst the raging onslaughts of Satan. No wonder— through Jesus, radical obedience is possible!

And so again, we come full circle. "But he answered, 'It is written, "One does not live by bread alone, but by every word that comes from the mouth of God"'" (Matthew 4:4). The secret to Christ's radical obedience will ever be the secret to yours and mine, too.

"It is written." Which means it is obvious that Jesus' own life was steeped in and saturated by the Word of God. "I treasure your word in my heart, so that I may not sin against you" (Psalm 119:11). That long-ago memory verse from childhood days still tells the truth, doesn't it? It clearly was what enabled Jesus to withstand the attacks of Satan.

And it will be what enables the Jesus Generation to withstand the final onslaught in the end. Here at last will be a generation of people who experientially will know and live the truth: "Without a personal acquaintance with Christ, and a continual communion, we are at the mercy of the enemy, and shall do his bidding in the end" (Ibid.). Here will be a people who, in longing to be like Jesus, will pray like Jesus and ask the Father for the Spirit like Jesus. They will be a generation of human beings whose deepest passion is to know God and Jesus Christ whom He sent (see John 17:3).

The Jesus Generation will live their contemporary, embattled lives in the context of their daily friendship with Christ. "It is written" for them will represent repeated devotional journeys through the life of Jesus in the gospels (and in *The Desire of Ages*). By beholding the radical obedience of Jesus, which He himself had to learn, they will become changed into His likeness. And His radical obedience will become theirs by daily faith and active pursuit.

It *must* become theirs. For I remind you that the wilderness showdown will happen one more time at the end of time. "At this the dragon grew furious with the woman, and went off to wage war on the rest of her offspring, that is, on those who keep God's commandments and maintain their testimony to Jesus" (Revelation 12:17, NEB).

Please note that in this final apocalyptic wilderness

showdown, nothing will have changed! The same furious dragon. The same blazing battleground. The same eternal stakes. And the same winning strategy. "But they conquered [the dragon] by the blood of the Lamb and by the word of their testimony" (Revelation 12:11). In the blood-dipped banner of Calvary, the Jesus Generation will find their mighty assurance of victory over Satan. For them the issue will never be reduced to, How much sinning can we get away with and still be saved? To sin or not to sin remains the choice; to trust or not to trust. And under the scarlet ensign of the cross, this end-time generation will stand in radical obedience to the Lamb—their Savior and their Lord.

Does that make the Jesus Generation perfect? No. But it does make them very much like the Lexus. Anybody who pays attention to the wonders of the automotive world knows that the Lexus is the crown jewel of the Toyota Motor Company. I have owned three Toyotas in my life, but I can assure you that I shall never have the good fortune of owning a Lexus! Their advertising agency developed a masterful marketing strategy for the nation. In an effort to proclaim their preeminence in the luxury car market, they chose as their motto: "Lexus—the relentless pursuit of perfection."

The relentless pursuit of perfection.

There will be a generation at the end of time just like Lexus, with its relentless pursuit of perfection. Only they won't be looking to Lexus; they will be looking instead to Jesus. And by beholding Him, they become changed into the likeness of Him who alone is perfect. But in the end, it will be enough for them to be like Jesus.

Trust and obey, for there's no other way to be just like Jesus, than to trust and obey.

7

"Heaven Can Weight"

The title's clever play on words caught my eye: "Heaven Can Weight." But what really got my attention was the subtitle to this feature article in *The Detroit News*! "Our religion writer converts to a healthy diet by taking a cue from the Adventists."

What follows is the opening salvo to Kate DeSmet's piece:

> One day, on an assignment as *The Detroit News'* religion writer, I asked children what kind of food God eats. "He goes to McDonald's," one girl shouted. "Lots of ice cream," said another. And one plump little boy replied: "He eats hamburgers and french fries for breakfast because His mother lets Him."
>
> If this is true, I wonder, is God, like so many of us, overweight? And if He is, does His doctor yell

at Him like mine did recently when he spotted my
20 extra pounds?

To anyone on a diet, losing fat can become a holy
cause. For me, just covering the church has been
pound-enhancing. Sitting in Catholic pews, eating
Episcopal Convention food and spending after-
noons in Pentecostal churches—then rushing to
file a story on deadline—gets you right in the gut.

When my doctor first read the fat facts on my
chart, he laughed aloud (there's a special place in
eternity's hottest kitchen for people who do that).
Then, like a preacher who knows he's got the sinner cornered, he lowered the boom and pre-
scribed my penance: Lose the weight, he told me,
and start exercising NOW!

Getting my doctor to yell at me was a good start.
But I also needed a blinding-light type experience,
something akin to what happened to St. Paul on
the road to Damascus. It occurred a month later
when I came across a new book called *The Seventh-
Day Diet*, (Random House, $19).

The book's cover said it was a plan for healthful
eating and weight loss by the Seventh-Day [sic] Adventists, "America's healthiest people." The divine
symmetry of it was stunning. Who better to help
an overweight religion writer than *the country's
healthiest religious denomination*? (*The Detroit News*,
June 11, 1991, emphasis supplied.)

Quite a testimony! But did you catch that accolade, "the
country's healthiest religious denomination"? But is she
right? Why, reading her article, you'd think Seventh-day
Adventists all have appetite licked. But do they—do we?
  Did you know that appetite and horses are a lot alike?
And that's not only when we eat like horses, either!

Whenever we take our kids up to beautiful Camp Au Sable in northern Michigan, they always clamor to go horseback riding. So I take them. I wish I could testify that I did so cheerfully, but I'll admit that I can't seem to get the hang of the rhythm of horseback riding. Every time the horse's gait is coming up, I'm going down. And when he's going down, I'm heading up, out of my stirrups! Which really messes up one's internal plumbing!

But I do know something about horse riding that Brenton Bullock, the Au Sable camp corral manager, taught me. The secret to successful riding is in the reins. Always keep the reins in your hands, and keep a slight tension on them. You aren't supposed to drop the reins and give the horse "free rein," which is where that phrase came from. The horse has been trained to obey the reins: Pull to the right, he turns in that direction; pull left, he veers left; pull back with a "Whoa!" and he slows up. You've got to rein a horse in.

And that makes a horse very much like appetite. Neither horses nor appetites must be allowed to **reign** (like a king); instead they must be **reined** (like a horse). Just like a horse, our appetites must be trained by reining them in. No reins—and appetite will reign. And like a wild stallion, it could end up trampling you to death!

In fact, more people on this planet are trampled to death by their own out-of-control appetites than by any other man-made disaster.

■ **Alcoholism**—you can die from that—is appetite out of control.

■ **AIDS**—you can die from that—is most often the result of appetite out of control.

■ **Smoking**—you can die from that—is the result of appetite out of control.

■ **Addictions** (of all kinds)—you can die from them—are the results of appetites out of control.

■ **Obesity** — you can die from that — is most often the result of appetite out of control.

■ **Gluttony** — you can die from that, too — is appetite out of control.

■ **Pornography** — you can die from that — is appetite out of control.

■ **Pride and self-worship** — you can die from them, too — are the results of appetite out of control.

In fact, could it be that every ill and evil afflicting our civilization can be traced to appetite out of control?

So it is no mere coincidence that when Lucifer decided to attack the incarnate God after His forty days of fasting, he picked appetite as his frontal assault!

> Jesus, full of the Holy Spirit, returned from the Jordan [after His baptism] and was led by the Spirit in the wilderness, where for forty days he was tempted by the devil. He ate nothing at all during those days, and when they were over, he was famished. (Luke 4:1, 2.)

Commenting on Lucifer's first wilderness temptation for Jesus, *The Desire of Ages* observes:

> Of all the lessons to be learned from our Lord's first great temptation none is more important than that bearing upon the control of the appetites and passions. In all ages, temptations appealing to the physical nature have been most effectual in corrupting and degrading mankind. Through intemperance [an old word for lack of self-control], Satan works to destroy the mental and moral power that God gave to man as a priceless endowment. The uncontrolled indulgence and consequent disease and degradation that existed at Christ's first advent will again exist, with intensity

of evil, before His second coming. . . . Upon the
very verge of that fearful time we are now living,
and to us should come home the lesson of the Saviour's fast. (Page 122.)

And what is the lesson of Jesus' fast? Appetite must not
reign; it must be reined.

So getting straight to the point of this chapter, maybe it's
time for the Jesus Generation to get serious about appetite,
so that rather than *reigning over* them, it will be *reined within*
them. Maybe to be like Jesus means to eat like Jesus. Maybe
the time has come for an end-time generation to rethink its
dietary habits. Because maybe there's more than meets the
eye to *The Detroit News* article.

Take *The New York Times*, for example. On April 23,
1992, it ran a full-page ad sponsored by a consortium of
ecology activists called "Beyond Beef Coalition." That explains the giant headline: "The Goal: A 50% Reduction of
Beef Consumption by 2002." The lengthy small-print article
began:

From a global viewpoint, one of the gravest
threats to the Earth's ecology, as well as to human
health, is the overconsumption of beef. Now, for
the first time in history, ecology groups are joining
animal protection, anti-hunger, human rights, family farm and health groups to launch the first
worldwide campaign to reduce the population of
cattle and the consumption of beef. Please join us.
It will benefit your health and the planet too.
Here are eight reasons why.

The ad then listed the eight reasons for abandoning the
consumption of beef and provided supportive data to cor-
roborate each reason: personal health, animal suffering,
rain forest destruction, global warming, water pollution and
scarcity, desertification (the diminishing of food-growing
land), world hunger, and the preservation of family farms.

This listing may not rank with your own ecological con-
cerns, but consider for a moment their number one reason:
personal health. Their supporting data caught my attention:

> The U.S. Surgeon General has reported that 70%
> of deaths in the United States are related to diet,
> especially the overconsumption of beef and other
> saturated fats. Americans now eat 25% of all the
> beef consumed in the world, a habit that all repu-
> table research has linked to heart disease, colon
> and breast cancers and strokes. Foreign countries
> that have lately adopted American diets have
> shown similar accelerating disease rates. *Aside
> from smoking, there is no greater personal health risk
> than eating meat.* (Ibid., emphasis supplied.)

No greater risk to your personal health, outside of
smoking, than eating meat? An astounding assertion, is it
not?

Interestingly, a growing coalition of voices around the
planet is now calling for the abandonment of meat eating!
Not only for scientific and dietary reasons, either. Major
cases are now being made based on ethical, as well as
ecological and economic principles. What Americans con-
sume is indeed a moral issue, these voices cry out!

That's why the Humane Farming Association took out a
full-page ad in *Newsweek* magazine. Headline: "Q: Why
can't this veal calf walk?" Below the headline, a black-and-
white photograph of a black-and-white calf chained in a
barn stall. The ad went on: "A: He has only two feet." Only
two feet? I counted at least three in the picture. The ad
continued now in small print:

> Actually, *less* than two feet. Twenty two inches
> to be exact. His entire life is spent chained in a
> wooden crate measuring only 22 inches wide
> and 56 inches long. The crate is so small the calf
> can't walk or even turn around. Most people

think animal abuse is illegal. It isn't. In veal factories, it's business as usual. "Milk-fed" veal is produced by making a calf anemic. The calf is *not* fed
mother's milk. He's fed an antibiotic-laced for-
mula that leads to diarrhea. He must lie in his
own excrement—choking on the ammonia gases
. . . . To keep calves alive under such torturous con-
ditions, they are given drugs which can be passed
on to consumers. (*Newsweek*, September 21, 1992.)

While it is obvious that these animal rights activists will
play their case to the gruesome hilt, it still is cause for
wonder, perhaps even alarm, isn't it? Ethically, ecologi-
cally, economically—if the case against meat eating is being
built in the secular press on those premises, it makes you
wonder what case the Jesus Generation can make for
reining in the appetite when it comes to the consumption
of flesh food or animal meat?

Maybe the time has come for the Jesus Generation to
exert new or renewed control over its appetite for animal
flesh. Do you suppose the time has come for a total fasting
from flesh food for the rest of our lives? Two separate
full-page ads declare that we would have nothing to lose
and very much to gain were we all to adopt such a radical
but rational stance.

But one does not live by ads alone. So look instead at
Jesus during His own grueling fast in that forty-day wilderness battle with Lucifer. Here is the incarnate God on a
mission to save a dying planet. It makes you wonder—if
such radical reining in of His appetite was important for
Jesus, how important do you suppose appetite control will
be for the end-time Jesus Generation? Will their appetites
be reigning over them or be reined within them?

If you're a vegetarian, it wouldn't be surprising if at this
point you're patting yourself on the back and commending
the dietary choice you've already made. And while I certainly do not wish to denigrate your choice, isn't it also true
that appetite and healthful living concern much more than

simply abstinence from animal flesh? But alas, the minute we raise the issue about that "much more," someone is bound to start muttering something about "gone from preachin' to meddlin'."

But then again, maybe it is time for the Jesus Generation to rein in its appetite for an alarmingly high usage and intake of sugar, fat, and cholesterol. And while nobody wants to go on record advocating total fasting and abstinence from the sweet chocolate delicacies and scrumptious ("scrumpdeli-icious," as Dennis the Menace touts for Dairy Queen) culinary concoctions that delight the human taste buds, nutritionists are building a thoroughly researched and significant case for controlled, reduced, and moderated usage of such "food" items. Obesity and gluttony are not only endemic nationally; they also represent very present battles for the Jesus Generation.

Winston Craig, professor of nutrition at Andrews University, in his 1992 book, *Nutrition for the Nineties*, has devoted over 300 pages to a dietary strategy for contemporary survival. Describing the typical American's diet— which annually includes consumption of 85 pounds of fat, 10 pounds of salt and 100 pounds of sugar, corn syrup and other sweeteners—Craig notes:

> Since so few of our calories come from grains, fruit, vegetables, and legumes it should come as no surprise that six of the top ten leading causes of death in the United States are associated with a faulty diet . . . . diets that are too high in fat, calories, cholesterol, sugar, salt, . . . and too low in fiber-rich foods. (Page 9.)

Can you be a teetotaling, non-smoking vegetarian and still be at risk?

Yes. While both Kate DeSmet (in "Heaven Can Weight") and Winston Craig quote national studies of Adventists (Craig notes over 200 scientific papers devoted to the health status of this group) showing that "the dietary habits of

Adventists enable them to enjoy lower mortality rates and an increased life expectancy" (Craig, p. 24), there are still potential risks that face members of this much-studied group. Notice the findings of Dr. L. Breslow, and run a mental checklist of your own lifestyle:

> Dr. Breslow identified seven specific health habits that were associated with good health. These included abstinence from alcohol and tobacco [two checks for your lifestyle list?], not eating between meals [wasn't there once a generation among us brought up to strictly adhere to the no-in-between-meals rule?], not sleeping too little or too much, having adequate exercise [oops!], having ideal body weight [well . . .], and eating a regular breakfast [who has time for a check here!]. (Craig, p. 27.)

So, how did your checklist go? Take a look at the corroborating evidence if you need to be convinced:

> Regular exercise had a greater effect on life expectancy than any other factor. Exercise is a natural tranquilizer and helps to reduce both stress and the risk of heart disease and high blood pressure. A typical 60 year-old individual who followed all seven of these health habits had the health of a 30 year-old person who followed less than three health habits. Those who followed all seven health principles had a life expectancy 11.5 years greater than those who followed three or less of them. (Ibid.)

But really, when it's all said and done, we need to remind ourselves that concern for our diet and control of our appetite are more than simply a matter of physical survival. They are just as much a vital condition for spiritual survival. A woman who wrote volumes a century ago would often write about diet. Why? Her perspective was not the longevity of the physical heart as much as it was the longevity of the spiritual one. Describing as she frequently did the great cosmic battle and struggle for human allegiance, she saw in the human mind the command center for every man, woman, and child.

> It is not mimic battles in which we are engaged. We are waging a warfare upon which hang eternal results. We have unseen enemies to meet. Evil angels are striving for the dominion of every human being. Whatever injures the health, not only lessens physical vigor, but tends to weaken the mental and moral powers. Indulgence in any unhealthful practice makes it more difficult for one to discriminate between right and wrong, and hence more difficult to resist evil. (*The Ministry of Healing*, p. 128.)

So Ellen White championed the theological concept of holistic living and repeatedly taught the symbiotic and sympathetic relationship that exists within body, mind, and spirit.

> Let it ever be kept before the mind that the great object of hygienic reform is to secure the highest possible development of mind and soul and body. All the laws of nature—which are the laws of God—are designed for our good. Obedience to them will promote our happiness in this life, and will aid us in a preparation for the life to come. (*Counsels on Diet and Foods*, p. 23.)

Our bodies and our souls are bound together—what you do to one will affect the other. If you and I are serious about the God we walk with, we'll be serious about the menu we eat from and the lifestyle we engage in!

> You need clear, energetic minds, in order to appreciate the exalted character of the truth [the Scriptures], to value the atonement [the cross], and to

place a right estimate upon eternal things. If you pursue a wrong course, and indulge in wrong habits of eating, and thereby weaken the intellectual powers, you will not place that high estimate upon salvation and eternal life which will *inspire you to conform your life to the life of Christ.* (Ibid., p. 47, emphasis supplied.)

For an end-time generation that seeks to be like Jesus, the matter of personal health and a controlled appetite cannot be ignored. It is a law of the spiritual realm that uncontrolled appetite is a symptom of an out-of-control life. Over and over, the New Testament appeals to its reader to sacredly care for his own health and resolutely rein in her own appetite.

What! Don't you know that your body is a temple of the Holy Spirit within you, and that you are not your own? For you were bought with a price; therefore glorify God in your body. (1 Corinthians 6:19, 20.)

Calvary is God's crimson price tag for saving you and me—body, mind, and spirit. Bought with a blood-stained price, we can know with certainty that how we treat our bodies and how we regard our health is a great moral issue of our times! We don't need newspaper articles or empirical research to prove that; the life of our Lord—forty days in the wilderness and a single day on an old rugged cross—is proof enough.

And that is the Good News. Because His victory on our behalf is not only about the price He paid, it is also about the power He promises! "For the message about the cross is foolishness to those who are perishing, but to us who are being saved it is the power of God" (1 Corinthians 1:18).

And it is that promise of power that is critical for the Jesus Generation. Lucifer's continuing onslaught against their appetites will only intensify as the end approaches.

But the Apocalypse rings with that clarion note of triumph for this end-time generation, "They have conquered [Lucifer] by the blood of the Lamb and by the word of their testimony, for they did not cling to life even in the face of death" (Revelation 12:11)! Their victory is assured—as sure as the victory of Jesus on the cross.

But the last phrase of that verse, "even in the face of death," is an apocalyptic reminder that when it comes to the power of appetite, nobody said it was going to be a piece of cake! (Jesus' forty days in the wilderness make that clear enough.) There are times in life when the necessary response to appetite is both radical and immediate—times when you can't afford to taper it off or slow it down, times when you simply must cut it out!

Petru Dumitriu, Russian author of *Incognito*, tells the story of a forester. In those Eurasian forests, long wooden chutes had been built on the hillside to slide tree-trunks down the slope to the valley and into the river. They were hundreds of yards long—smooth, polished inside, and very slippery. So much so that the foresters would sit on the floor of the chute or on an axe-handle, and they'd go tobogganing down the chute to save themselves the trouble of walking.

As one forester was sliding his way down to the valley floor one day, the man's foot got caught in a hole in the chute, and he couldn't get it free. As he struggled to release his foot, he froze as he heard a shout of warning from atop the hill which signaled that a tree-trunk was on its thundering way down the express chute.

The forester turned and saw the thing coming straight for him. His foot was jammed; he couldn't free it. So with the split second remaining, he hacked his foot off with his axe and jumped clear just in time. As Dumitriu put it, he was crippled for life, but at least he was alive.

How did Jesus put it? "If your hand or your foot causes you to stumble; cut it off. And if your eye causes you to stumble, tear it out. For it is better for you to enter life maimed or lame or blind, than to have two hands or two feet or two eyes and be lost in the end" (see Matthew 18:8, 9). So it is with appetite. If it is causing you to stumble—whatever it is—haven't you come to the right time to cut it off and give it up?

"Heaven can weight" . . . for *The Detroit News* writer Kate De Smet, perhaps. But heaven can't wait forever for you and me. Eternity is too high a price to pay for something from which Jesus can set you free, if you ask Him today. He's already paid the eternal price; and He's ready to give His eternal power. Why don't you ask Him now? You don't have to wait any longer.

8

A Destiny in Mothballs

In 1923 a meeting of the financial world's *creme de la creme*—the economic movers and shakers of society—took place in the Edgewater Beach Hotel in the Windy City of Chicago. At that famous gathering were nine of the world's most successful financiers.

I found in the book *Ministry* a list of the individuals in attendance that day: the president of the largest independent steel company, the president of the largest utility company, the president of the largest gas company, the greatest wheat speculator, the president of the New York Stock Exchange, a member of the president's cabinet, the greatest bear on Wall Street, the head of the world's greatest monopoly, and finally, the president of the Bank of International Settlements. Talk about a high-powered convocation! Assembled here were the "supreme masters of the financial universe."

Twenty-five years later, in 1948, how dramatically the

picture has changed! Charles Schwab has died bankrupt after living on borrowed money for the last five years of his life. Samuel Insull has died a fugitive from justice, penniless in a foreign land. Howard Hopson has gone insane. Arthur Critten has died abroad, insolvent. Richard Whitney has just been released from Sing Sing, the federal penitentiary. Albert Fall has been pardoned from prison so he can die at home. Jesse Livermore has committed suicide, as has Leon Fraser and Ivar Kreuger. Nine masters of finance who were mastered in the end by their own wealth.

What might we learn from their tragic endings?

> The extraordinary sameness of the hellish gravity
> of their famous lives is a divine warning, for God
> set the ghosts of these financial giants as spectral,
> mid-century witnesses to a nation about to run
> amok in materialism. Today their ghosts have
> faded, and a new gallery of forlorn spirits is assem-
> bling. (*Ministry*, p. 173.)

Aren't you glad you're not rich—at least not as rich as they were! Come on now, be honest. Right now you're probably thinking to yourself: Well, if you want me to be honest, I will—the answer is, No I'm not **glad** I'm not rich . . . I'm **mad** and **sad** I'm not rich! I mean, I do feel bad for these nine fellas. But the way I've got it figured is, Just try me! I know I'd do better with all that money than they did! After all, it isn't fair—so much money in the world, and I get so little of it!

I suppose we all could confess to some such ruminations deep within us on occasions in the not-too-distant past. Especially whenever we've read the news media's latest reporting of superstar salaries! I heard the news a few days ago about Michael Eisner, CEO of Walt Disney, who was reported to have exercised his stock options to the tune of between $100 to $150 million profit before taxes.

Forbes magazine recently released its annual ranking of the world's highest-paid athletes. And guess what? The

Gatorade star, Michael Jordan, topped the list with a $3.9 million salary for 1992! Add to that his earnings from product endorsements (like Gatorade), which were estimated at $32 million last year, and you have Michael Jordan's grand-total earnings in 1992 at $35.9 million! (We should have gone into basketball, right?) And while I don't want to denigrate his well-earned superstar status, something does seem to be a bit askew in terms of economic parity in this world, doesn't it?

Forbes went on to list the others in this top-ten ranking: Evander Holyfield (boxing), Ayrton Senna (auto racing), Nigel Mansell (auto racing), Arnold Palmer (golf), Andre Agassi (tennis), Joe Montana (football), Jack Nicklaus (golf), Jim Courier (tennis), and Monica Seles (tennis) at the bottom of the list with earnings in 1992 of only $8.5 million!

So it is only natural for us to exclaim—Don't give me this business about, Aren't you glad you're not rich? 'Cause I'm mad and sad I'm not rich!

But wait a minute. You are rich, are you not? Remember Somalia? Remember that barrage of disturbing video and print images we were bombarded with not very long ago? Pull one of those pictures back up in your memory for a moment. Gaze uncomfortably again into the bloodshot, haunted eyes of that little girl the *Newsweek* photographer captured in his December 7, 1992, photo essay of human suffering. Her age, six or seven perhaps—that little girl who stares back at you and me in the ghoulish colors of her tragedy. She is little more than a bone-protruding specter of grotesquely stretched skin on her forlorn little skeleton. And a tear trickles down her bony, hollow face. For she is a living victim of the slow death of human starvation—a photographic statistic we've become tragically too familiar with of late around this planet, be it Bosnia or Somalia.

But gaze into her impoverished and emaciated countenance, and then tell me you are not rich and increased with goods! The problem is, we've been using the wrong paradigms to define wealth and poverty. Forget Michael Jordan and Michael Eisner, whose much-heralded wealth is an obscene shame for this nation's value system. Why don't we let the abject poverty of Somalia become the paradigm for defining our own economic station on this planet? If we do, then you are rich, and so am I. Even if you back Somalia out of the picture and end up with only a box of cowfeed in a long-ago Bethlehem manger, we are still rich—very, very rich.

How does the Christmas story go? "And she gave birth to her firstborn son and wrapped him in bands of cloth, and laid him in a manger, because there was no place for them in the inn" (Luke 2:7). It simply defies our logic and boggles our minds—that the God of the universe would incarnate Himself in a human womb for nine months! And get this—NOT the human womb of the Empress of Rome, either. He chose instead the tender young womb of a dirt-poor girl in an obscure backwater village called Nazareth. You can't possibly pick a more impoverished birthplace than a stinking barnyard cow stall! The King of the Universe born in a barn (the very place our parents hinted we too were born, judging from our occasional boorish manners)!

The Queen of England was embarrassingly much in the news not long ago. With her annual salary of $12 million, her personal fortune is estimated variously at $1.5 to $10 billion, all of it tax free, creating quite a furor among the citizens of her kingdom. And it all came to a head with the tragic Windsor Castle fire. Who should pay for the losses— the wealthiest woman in the world or her people? As you know, a compromise was reached, and life goes in the kingdom.

But even the Queen of England with her Croesus-like wealth is but a paltry and pitiful comparison to the divine Monarch of a trillion galaxies! That the supreme Creator God of all life would humble Himself to be born in a foul, dank cow stall is truly incomprehensible. Animal crackers for the King of heaven!

Archbishop Fulton J. Sheen, in his classic *Life of Christ*, penned it well:

> There was no room in the inn, but there was room in the stable. The inn is the gathering place of public opinion, the focal point of the world's moods, the rendezvous of the worldly, the rallying place of the popular and the successful. But the stable is a place for the outcasts, the ignored, the forgotten. The world might have expected the Son of God to be born—if He was to be born at all—in an inn. A stable would be the last place in the world where one would have looked for Him. *Divinity is always where one least expects to find it."* (Page 28, emphasis his.)

You see, we have it all wrong. We think the bumper sticker is true: "The one with the most toys wins." So if we were God, we'd have never shown up at some stinking back-alley cave. Ah, but Fulton Sheen is right: *"Divinity is always where one least expects to find it."* For who would have thought you'd find the Almighty God by checking the barnyards of Bethlehem?

It is the story of Christmas poverty. We know the story well—too well. And that's the problem. That is why it no longer captures our fancy or captivates our wonder. Which is why it's time we read the story somewhere else. In fact, here is the most powerful, the most poignant one-line summation of Christmas you'll ever read. "For you know the generous act of our Lord Jesus Christ, that though he was rich, yet for your sakes he became poor, so that by his poverty you might become rich" (2 Corinthians 8:9). Remember the poor little girl from Somalia? Read Paul's words again. "For you know the generous act of our Lord Jesus Christ, that though he was rich, yet for your sakes he became poor, so that by his poverty you might become rich." The portrait of poverty.

He became poor, so that by His self-sacrifice you and I

might be richly saved. Come on, friend, what are you and I supposed to do with the story of Christmas—the story of a God who entered into such radical self-sacrifice, all for the likes of you and me? And what do you think the Jesus Generation will do with such a story? That generation of men and women and children living at the end of time—what will they do with this story of God's radical self-sacrifice?

I have a feeling I know the answer, and I predict you do, too. What the Jesus Generation will do is bind this one-liner *about* Jesus with a one-liner *from* Jesus. And by so doing, they will turn this theological statement into an ethical imperative.

Because they well remember the words of Jesus in Matthew 10:8: "Freely you have received, freely give" (KJV). And it really is a very simple union, when they join Matthew's line from Jesus with Paul's line about Jesus. "For you know the generous act of our Lord Jesus Christ, that though he was rich, yet for your sakes he became poor, so that by his poverty you might become rich." "Freely you have received; freely give." Which being interpreted means—As you have been saved by radical sacrifice, so you must live by radical sacrifice. How you've been saved is how you must live.

And that is why the Jesus Generation has been called to radical sacrifice. Not as some sort of punishment by God— not as some sort of "if-it-tastes-bad-it-must-be-good-for-you" remedy from Him. But rather, as a deep, welling, spontaneous gratitude to the God who became radically impoverished so that we might become eternally enriched.

Call it a sense of grateful indebtedness, if you want. James Denny, in *Death of Christ*, observes: "I do not hesitate to say that the sense of debt to Christ is the most profound and pervasive of all emotions in the New Testament" (p. 158). It is a sense of indebtedness to the One whose radical sacrifice has truly made us rich.

John Stott illustrates it this way in his book *The Cross of Christ*:

If you were to jump off the end of a pier and drown, or dash into a burning building and be burnt to death, and if your self-sacrifice had no saving purpose, you would convince me of your folly, not your love. But if I were myself drowning in the sea, or trapped in the burning building, and it was in attempting to rescue me that you lost your life, then I would indeed see love not folly in your action. (Page 220.)

When you gaze into the crimson face of Calvary and realize that ultimate self-sacrifice was for you—He did it for *me*—when this realization truly penetrates the human psyche so that you gratefully accept and embrace this indescribable gift from God, the utterly profound emotion is indeed a sense of debt to Christ!

And the consequent response is equally predictable. Let's say, using Stott's illustration, you were the one who died in an attempt to save my life (whether you jumped off a pier or ran into a blazing inferno). Will I not be devoted to the memory of your self-sacrifice for the rest of my life?

And let's say you left behind a poor, struggling family. Don't you think that out of eternal gratitude for your sacrificial act, it would be a small thing for me to express my indebtedness to your memory by sacrificing my own meager wares and means in order to help provide for the needs of your surviving, struggling loved ones? Why, of course I would make such a sacrifice—and so would you, if the tables were turned!

Let's put it another way. William Barclay, the New Testament commentator, wrote a sentence that I have carried on the flyleaf of my Bible for some years now: "A man must give his life to that which gave him life." There is a lot to reflect upon in that single line. For what is it that has given you life today? Whatever it is, give your life for it in return.

"For you know the generous act of our Lord Jesus Christ,

that though he was rich, yet for your sakes he became poor, so that by his poverty you might become rich." "Freely you have received; freely give."

For the Jesus Generation, there is no equivocation over what gave them life. And so the radical sacrifice of Jesus for them summons their radical sacrifice for Him. "Freely you have received; freely give."

That, in fact, is the great and shining principle of Christian stewardship. The word we all love to hate: *stewardship.* But if it bothers you, forget the word; just remember the way. As you have been saved by radical sacrifice, so live by radical sacrifice. How you have been saved is how you must live. Joyful sacrifice.

And it is intended to be joyful, you know—this cheerful, sacrificial giving of our means, giving of our time, giving of our abilities for the sake and service of Christ. It is a joyful kind of sacrificing—a grateful returning to the One who made it all possible in the first place.

Which leads me to suggest that if this thought of radical sacrifice is going to make you mad, forget it! God doesn't need it. He doesn't need our means or our time or our abilities or talents. After all, He is the owner of the cattle on a thousand hills (and the hills underneath the cattle, from the latest reports we've received), and all the silver and the gold of this planet is His! (See Psalm 50:10 and Haggai 2:8.) So if sacrificing a portion of them back to God is going to make you grumble and gripe, forget it!

He'll find some widow with two mites, when the rich young rulers walk away and refuse to sacrifice. He'll call some poor illiterate fisher folk, if the brilliant ecclesiastics and academicians don't have time for Him. Because it's true, "God loves a cheerful giver" (2 Corinthians 9:7). He really does love cheerful followers and cheerful givers.

Now please don't think me impertinent, but it occurs to me that God has got to love a place like the parish and the community where I live and pastor—a place that offers a hundred ways for young and old to give of themselves in cheerful, radical sacrifice. Come to think of it, God must love the church and community you belong to, too!

You *do* belong to a congregation, don't you? Why, it would be impossible to define the Jesus Generation, if it were simply a nebulous, ethereal communion of human beings united only by their theology and ideology! Yes, of course, the Jesus Generation is a community of faith bonded by the great themes and truths of the Holy Scriptures. But beyond theology and ideology is the reality of ecclesiology—the vibrant truth about the church! And the consistent New Testament witness is of a worshiping and working community of faith—senior citizens, middle-aged adults, young adults, teenagers, and children joined together by their shared passion for Christ and devotion to His kingdom. Only such a working and worshiping community of faith could possibly fulfill the scriptural admonition:

> And let us consider how to provoke one another
> to love and good deeds, not neglecting to meet to-
> gether, as is the habit of some, but encouraging
> one another, and all the more as you see the Day
> approaching. (Hebrews 10:24, 25.)

The approaching Day is nearly here! With the rampant evidence of a soon-coming Jesus torched across the façade of contemporary society, now more than ever the Jesus Generation must be a community of passionate faith, efficiently organized and effectively operating in a shared mission to reach this dying planet quickly. To subscribe to the notion that all you really need is a clearly defined theology and then you can go it alone, is a foolhardy enterprise.

Dwight L. Moody was calling on the home of a gentleman who had long since quit attending the local congregation. The man rather confidently bantered with Moody that some people don't need the church and its cumbersome and oftimes awkward communal relations. "I have Jesus, and that's all that matters," the man asserted. Moody listened. And when the gentleman had finished, Moody quietly took the fireplace tongs and poked a burning ember away from the crackling fire and out onto the cold hearth. The two men sat there in silence as the once bright and fiery ember, separated now from the fire, slowly but surely began to fade, until in the end it was nothing but a dark, cold lump of ash.

As weak and inefficient (and sometimes, I'll admit, ineffective) as the body of Christ can be, the fact remains that for the Jesus Generation, the church will continue to be Christ's chosen instrument to keep His fiery love and His burning mission alive on this earth. To pull away from this spiritual community with the complaint that your local congregation is too inept or too small or simply too irrelevant is to miss the very point of "church." How many times have you and I heard the muttering, "But I don't get anything out of church anymore." But that's just it. For you see, church has much less to do with getting out of and much more to do with giving into! Small urban congregations and struggling rural parishes may not boast a Robert Schuller kind of entertainment. They may not even be like the church you attended while in college. But this much I do know. They are the kind of congregations that very much need what you have to give.

And I don't mean giving only in the financial context of stewardship. I think of all the volunteer organizations in our church and around our communities that desperately need us to share our time and our talents. The list must be a mile long. From the children's Sabbath School divisions in your own congregation (and every pastor knows that there will be a special place in heaven reserved for the unselfish men and women who gave themselves in this life so freely to the children of the church) to the Big Brother and Big Sister organizations of your town. From the Dorcas and Community Service Centers to the soup kitchens and health vans of the inner cities. From the Pathfinder Club to the Red Cross or hospital auxiliaries. You may not be able to be in Somalia, but you can be doing something for the homeless and the suffering right here in this country and in your county. "Freely you have received; freely give."

And yes, that does include the meager or the expansive wealth God has entrusted to you. For radical sacrifice, in order to be both radical and sacrificial, will permeate our portfolios and checkbooks and bank accounts. The Jesus Generation has been called to the most significant financial partnership with the Master in the history of this world. The unprecedented global needs that face us today (from the collapse of the Soviet republics to the burgeoning Third World challenge), the unrelenting local necessities that plead for our support (from the struggling church schools of our parishes to the mounting costs of keeping the local congregation going and growing)—all of these are urgent enough opportunities to join forces financially with God in reaching this civilization before the impending end.

If ever there were an hour for the Jesus Generation to invest its means and to liquidate its assets for the kingdom of heaven, isn't it now? It would be unconscionable for this end-time generation to be building castles in the sand when the sea is crashing in!

To change the metaphor, consider the mothball. Have you ever smelled a mothball? I don't know if many people even use them any more, but I can certainly recall their olfactory pungency! I remember our little summer vacation cabin on the hillside of an azure mountain lake in Japan. As a boy I lived for those unforgettable summertime weeks away from the hot, humid confines of Tokyo.

And the first smell that would greet us when we unlocked and unboarded our cabin was always the smell of the mothballs Mother had stashed away amidst all our summer linens and clothing. Perhaps you can still smell them, too. I guess those little white balls did the trick and really did keep the moths away. But I know I'll never forget their medicinal smell.

It's an odor I recall every time I hear Jesus speak those familiar words:

> Do not lay up for yourselves treasures on earth, where moth and rust consume and where thieves break in and steal; but store up for yourselves treasures in heaven, where neither moth nor rust consumes and where thieves do not break in and steal. For where your treasure is, there your heart will be also. (Matthew 6:19-21.)

The Jesus Generation isn't called to a destiny in mothballs. Through radical sacrifice, they are a people investing their treasures in eternity. Which is why they keep giving themselves and their treasures away. Which makes them very much like the Jesus they follow, from the manger to the cross. And when you're following Jesus, it isn't a sacrifice at all!

9

When Passion Is More Than a Kiss

I did a double-take when I read the headline in the Sunday paper: "Classic kiss photo subject of suit." Somebody's suing over a kiss?

Sure enough, the opening lines of the Associated Press release (datelined Paris) read: "Forty-two years after Robert Doisneau immortalized youthful love with the click of a camera, the celebrated photographer is being taken to court by an aging couple claiming he stole their kiss" (*South Bend Tribune*, December 6, 1992). It turned out that the hotly disputed kiss is the one captured in the famous 1950 photograph of Doisneau's entitled, "Le Baiser de l'Hotel de Ville" (The Kiss at City Hall).

The world fell in love with that black-and-white photograph of a young French couple caught in the embrace of a spontaneous, passionate kiss amid a crowd of strollers outside the Paris City Hall. Two lovers, oblivious to the passing world, lost in each other's kiss. The popular photograph has appeared on posters and T-shirts around the world. It is studied in schools as an example of the photographer's art.

But back in 1988 Denise and Jean-Louis Lavergne, a middle-aged couple running a printing shop in one of the working-class suburbs of Paris, saw the photograph for the first time. As it turned out, they were celebrating their thirty-eighth wedding anniversary that day. And when they picked up the magazine cover and recognized themselves— so they say—as the two lovers, they were thrilled! They wanted to meet Robert Doisneau, and in January 1990 the meeting took place over lunch. According to their recollections, he seemed as glad as they were to meet at last. "He was happy, kissed me, and asked 'Why don't I have news of you?'" Mrs. Lavergne recalled. The aged photographer then asked them to appear in a film being made for his eightieth birthday.

But when the film was aired on French television, the sequence with the Lavergnes was cut. And when associates of the famed photographer began giving interviews denying that the famous kiss belonged to the Lavergnes, the couple decided to sue.

"They say there is magic in that photo," Mrs. Lavergne, now 64 years of age, was quoted as saying. "That photo is a testament to our youth, and we regret that we're not being recognized." So to court they're all headed. According to the press release, a judge will decide the case within three months. So much for hotly disputed kisses!

Passion in a black-and-white photograph. (And apparently riches, too!) But then aren't we all—"brown and yellow, black and white"—creatures of passion? Why, to even speak the word awakens some deep and stirring chord within us, doesn't it? But what is there about passion that is so compelling? What are our passions?

After all, when we speak of passion, we often times are endeavoring to capture in a word some profound, powerful human emotion such as love or joy, hatred or anger. Passion can also be the way we describe the objects we fervently desire. Thus we speak of a person's passion for life or fast cars or rare art or gardening. David Hume, the Scottish philosopher, once wrote, "I was seized very early with a passion for literature, which has been the ruling passion of my life." Could it be that we all have those ruling passions?

Hans Küng, in his book *Why I Am Still a Christian*, describes it this way:

> We all have a personal God: *a supreme value by which we regulate everything, to which we orientate ourselves, for which if need be we sacrifice everything.* And if this is not the true God, then it is some kind of idol, an old or a new one—money, career, sex, or pleasure—none of them evil things in themselves, but enslaving for those for whom they become God. (Page 47, emphasis supplied.)

Küng is right. All of us have those ruling passions, those supreme values for which, if need be, we sacrifice everything.

So what do you suppose is God's passion? He does have passion, doesn't He? Can you imagine the very One who created us with such a deep, welling capacity for passion being bereft of passion Himself?

But what is the passion of God? Any response to that query must of necessity interface with the mystery of the incarnation (the "in-flesh-ment," as the Latin word means) of God within the human race. It strains our capacity for comprehension whenever we grapple with the notion of an infinite and eternal God becoming incarnated in the muck and mire of the human manger! Would an intelligent Being ever undertake such supreme condescension, were it not for a fiery and compelling passion?

So what is God's passion?

The Passion Shown

Reexamine the life of the incarnated One; look for a

moment at Jesus. There is a shimmering clue to the divine passion there in the noontide heat atop the lip of Jacob's well. You remember the story well—a story masterfully recaptured in a short book kindly given to me by some university students here in my parish. It is told so poignantly that I want to share Ken Gire's word picture in its entirety from his book, *Intimate Moments with the Savior*:

> The Palestine sun glares its impartial eye upon both this nameless Samaritan woman and upon the Savior of the world. Weary from travel, he stops to rest beside Jacob's well. She, too, is on her way to that well, keeping (unbeknown to her) an appointment with destiny. For *she* is the reason "he had to go through Samaria."
>
> Through sheer curtains of undulating heat she comes. She too is weary. Not so much from the water jar she carries on her head as from the emptiness she carries in her heart. The husked emptiness left over from the wild oats of years past.
>
> The torrents of passion, once swift in her life, have now run their course. She is weathered and worn, her face eroded by the gulleys [sic] of a spent life.
>
> That she comes at noon, the hottest hour of the day, whispers a rumor of her reputation. The other women come at dawn, a cooler, more comfortable hour. They come not only to draw water but to take off their veils and slip out from under the thumb of a male-dominated society. They come for companionship, to talk, to laugh, and to barter gossip—much of which centers around this woman. So, shunned by Sychar's wives, she braves the sun's scorn. Anything to avoid the searing stares of the more reputable.

For a span of five husbands she has come to this well. Always at noon. Always alone.

Accusing thoughts are her only companions as she ponders the futile road her life has traveled. She thinks back to the crossroads in her life, of roads that might have been taken, of happiness that might have been found. But she knows she can never go back.

She's at a dead end right now, living with a man in a relationship that leads nowhere. She knows that. But for now she needs him. His presence fills the lonely nights with a measured cup of companionship, however shallow or tepid.

She has gone from man to man like one lost in the desert, sun-struck and delirious. For her, marriage has been a retreating mirage. Again and again she has returned to the matrimonial well, hoping to draw from it something to quench her thirst for love and happiness. But again and again she has left that well disappointed.

As her eyes meet the Savior's, he sees within her a cavernous aching, a cistern in her soul that will forever remain empty unless he fills it. Through her eyes, he peers into her past with tenderness. He sees every burst of passion's flame . . . and every passion's burnt out failure.

Yet to her, an anonymous woman with a failed life, he gives the most profound discourse in Scripture on the subject of worship—that God is spirit and that worship is not an approach of the body to a church, but an approach of the soul to the spirit of God. A cutting revelation to one who has lived so much of her life in the realm of the physical rather than the spiritual.

But equally remarkable is what Jesus doesn't say. He states her past and present marital status but makes no reference to her sin. He gives no call to repent. He presents no structured plan of salvation. He offers no prayer.

What he does do is take her away from the city and bring her to a quiet well. There he shows her a reflection of herself. Understandably, she shrinks back.

She then takes a detour down the backroads of theology. But with the words "I who speak to you am he," Jesus brings her back to face the giver and his remarkable gift—living water. Not a wage to be earned. Not a prize to be won. But a gift to be received.

To her this stranger was first simply "a Jew" . . . then "Sir" . . . then "a prophet." Now she sees him for who he really is—"Messiah."

In that intimate moment of perception, she leaves to tell this good news to the city that has both shared her and shunned her. Behind, left in the sand, is her empty water jar. Stretching before her is a whole new life. And with her heart overflowing with living water she starts to run. Slowly at first. Then as fast as her new legs will take her. (Pages 23-25.)

Ken Gire's meditation ends here. But the Gospel of John adds a concluding vignette. And it is in this story's epilogue that we discover a shining clue to God's passion.

The Samaritan woman, on hearing the sound of approaching voices, has turned and run. The disciples, laden down from their fast-food, brown-bag mission to the village and hurrying back to enjoy their noontide repast with the

Master, raise their corporate eyebrows as the lady rushes past them. "They were astonished that he was speaking with a woman" (John 4:27).

But they are even more astonished when, with hungry anticipation, they crowd around Jesus and the well and begin to spread out their picnic lunch, only to have Jesus look up with a smile and shake His head. "I have food to eat that you do not know about," He says (verse 32). The whisper shoots through the picnickers, "Jesus has changed His mind—He isn't hungry any more!" You can almost hear the flabbergasted responses: "He isn't hungry? After all the work of trudging into town for food, He doesn't want any of it? Come on!" And with one voice they offer their health tip for the day, "Rabbi, eat something" (verse 31).

But Jesus quietly declines. He seems lost in reverie. "So the disciples said to one another, 'Surely no one has brought him something to eat?'" (verse 33). Jesus, sensing their perplexity, finally speaks. And when He does, we glimpse the passion of God. "My food is to do the will of him who sent me and to complete his work. Do you not say, 'Four months more, then comes the harvest'? But I tell you, look around you, and see how the fields are ripe for harvesting" (verses 34, 35). *The Desire of Ages* describes groups of Samaritans hurrying up the road to the well even as Jesus speaks of a harvest already come!

And there she is at the head of the crowd, this woman who brings her entire neighborhood to meet the Savior she has found. No wonder Jesus is no longer hungry! "I've had different food to eat, for my food is the passion of my Father in heaven."

What is the ruling passion of the incarnated God? What is it that can slake His thirst and stave off His hunger? Still not sure?

Remember the three famous stories of Christ—stories about a lost sheep and a lost coin and a lost son? Too often we skim over Luke's preface to those three parables and miss a key piece of evidence for discovering the divine passion.

> Now all the tax collectors and sinners were coming near to listen to [Jesus]. And the Pharisees and the scribes were grumbling and saying, This fellow welcomes sinners and eats with them." (Luke 15:1, 2.)

That two-line preface is a sermon in itself. What a paradox! Here are the Pharisees, who consider themselves paragons of virtue, and yet who throughout the gospel story appear to be so uncomfortable in Jesus' company. And on the other hand, here are all the social low-rung outcasts—the tax agents and the profligate and other such "sinners." And yet, throughout the gospels, they are spontaneously drawn to the Savior.

"This man welcomes sinners and eats with them!" Little do those grumbling, griping ecclesiastics realize that they in fact are declaring the greatest news in all history! That the sovereign and supreme God of the universe would descend to this rebel planet and pull up a chair to our sinner tables and eat with us! No wonder they call the gospel Good News!

Aren't you glad God isn't as snobbish as organized religion sometimes makes Him out to be? It doesn't matter who you are or what you've done—there is a passion in the heart of God for you, a longing to pull up a chair to your table and eat with you . . . just you and Him together. Because God knows that in that intimate encounter there is healing for the life, both now and forever. What a passion!

And then, just in case we still aren't sure of the passion, Luke lines up the three great parables to prove the passion's point. And did you notice, every time the lost is found, they throw a party! "Just so I tell you, there will be more joy in heaven over one sinner who repents than over ninety-nine righteous persons who need no repentance" (Luke 15:7).

And again, "Just so, I tell you, there is joy in the presence of the angels of God over one sinner who repents" (verse 10). And why not throw a party? "'Get the fatted calf and kill it, and let us eat and celebrate; for this son of mine was dead and is alive again; he was lost and is found!' And they began to celebrate" (verses 23, 24). Celebrate, indeed! No wonder John Newton called it "amazing grace"—"I once was lost but now am found!" God has a passion, alright! A passion to find the lost.

So that when Jesus was standing there in the glittering opulence of that ornate dining room in the home of the conniving, cheating, swindling, embezzling tax collector and sinner named Zacchaeus, He forever set the record straight regarding the ruling passion of the eternal and incarnate God: "For the Son of Man came to seek out and to save the lost" (Luke 19:10).

There it is in black and white—the passion that birthed the Christmas story and the Calvary story. Because whether you gaze upon the Bethlehem cradle or upon the Calvary cross, you can know that the tiny infant hands that grow up to be nailed to a Roman cross are hands stretched out for a single, solitary passion—to seek and save the lost. The passion of Christ was the premise of the cross, and of the cradle, too. "For the Son of Man came to seek out and to save the lost."

The Passion Shared

But, you see, God is not content only to **show** His passion to us. By His very nature, He longs to **share** His passion through us. That's why there is a Jesus Generation at the end of human history—a generation that has been called to share the passion of God for a dying planet. For when you know you've been loved that much, you can't sit forever on news that good, can you?

Which is why the last words—the very last words—Jesus spoke on earth were words that passed the passion on to us. There on the mount, He turned to His followers—and to you and me, as well—with the quiet command: "You will be my witnesses first in your hometown and then in your home state and then in your homeland and then throughout all the world. Go, for I am with you always, even to the end of the age" (see Acts 1:8 and Matthew 28:18, 19).

Did you catch that? "You will be my witnesses." And "witnesses" means passion! You may be thinking, There certainly is no passion in witnessing! But wait a minute. The Greek word for a "witness" is *martus*, from whence comes our word *martyr*. And who is a martyr? One who believes so deeply in something or someone that she is willing to give her life for it or him. And that is passion!

The Gospel Commission isn't commanding everybody to die for Jesus, but with a clarion summons, it is calling the Jesus Generation to live for Him! And how then shall we live? Live with His passion to seek and save the lost. For to be a follower of this same Jesus is to share in this same passion.

The problem is that we have blown the life of witnessing way out of proportion! So that 2,000 years later, we figure witnessing has something to do with six years of post-high school education, two degrees, and ordination before it can possibly be attempted. And if not that, then surely we must at least attend a few local seminars and national conferences before ever daring to become a "witness" for Jesus!" Has it come to that?

Can you imagine what a fix we'd all be in if we treated the passion of love in the same way! (The only ones who are allowed to love are those who have advanced degrees in love, or at least have taken a minimum of three seminars on love. All others need not apply!)

Do you suppose we're wrong about how the passion gets shared? Maybe it isn't about paid professionals at all! Maybe when the Spirit of Jesus fills your heart, there's a spontaneity and a freedom that lets you share Jesus' passion in a very natural, uncontrived sort of way.

Let's say we're both at a party together. You're moving

through the crowded room with a drink in your hand. As you're chatting your way through all the laughter and commotion, I accidentally bump into you. And your drink splashes all over the front of me! Forgetting for a moment our mutual embarrassment, let me ask you—What is it that spills out of your glass and onto me? The answer is obvious—naturally, whatever it is you have in your glass!

And that precisely is what witnessing is all about! When the Spirit of Jesus fills a man's heart, and he moves through the crowded marketplaces and crossroads of life and bumps into people, what spills out of him is what's inside of him.

When the Holy Spirit fills a woman's heart, and she moves through a hospital or an office and bumps into patients or colleagues or clients, what spills out of her is what's inside of her. That's what witnessing is all about.

When students are filled with the Spirit of Christ and move across their campus and through their dormitory bumping into classmates and professors, friends or strangers, what spills out of them is what's inside of them. That's what witnessing is all about.

"But you will receive power when the Holy Spirit comes on you, and you will be My witnesses" (Acts 1:8). That's not a demand; that's a delight. I have never known the sharing of a passion to be a bore. Just ask any lover, if you don't believe me!

That's why Hans Küng is right when he wrote:

> [Jesus] calls for personal discipleship. . . . That means I commit myself to him and pursue my own way in accordance with his direction. . . . It is not that we must. We are not compelled. Making his way our own was understood from the very beginning as a very great opportunity, not a "must" but a "may," not a law to be slavishly obeyed but an unexpected change and a true gift. (Ibid., p. 59.)

How did Jesus put it? "When you receive my gift, you

will be my witnesses." That is a promise. Because when the glass is filled and then bumped, it naturally splashes out onto the world around it. That is what witnessing is all about.

The Passion Seen

And will the world see and know this same Jesus by bumping into the Jesus Generation? Will they see Jesus, and will it make a difference? The answer to both questions, I believe, is Yes.

Take Malcolm X, for example. The assassinated leader of a movement to unite blacks around the world was recently much in the news again, thanks to the extensively touted release of the movie production of his life. But guess what? He knew Seventh-day Adventists.

Read these lines from his book, *The Autobiography of Malcolm X*:

> About this time, my mother began to be visited by some Seventh Day [sic] Adventists who had moved into a house not too far down the road from us. They would talk to her for hours at a time, and leave booklets and leaflets and magazines for her to read. She read them. . . .

> Before long, my mother spent much time with the Adventists. . . . We began to go with my mother to the Adventist meetings that were held further out in the country. For us children, I know that the major attraction was the good food they served. But we listened, too. There were a handful of Negroes, from small towns in the area, but I would say that it was ninety-nine percent white people. The Adventists felt that we were living at the end of time, that the world soon was coming to an end. *But they were the friendliest white people I had ever seen.* (Pages 16, 17, emphasis supplied.)

The friendliest people in town? I don't know whom Malcolm X met, but I'm sure glad he met them! Don't you wish they'd say that about your hometown and mine? "Those Adventists have got to be the friendliest church, the friendliest people in town!"

Isn't that what the Jesus Generation is all about—reflecting Jesus' pro-active love and His unselfish caring, one human being at a time, until the world shines with His glory? You don't need an advanced degree in living the love of Jesus in your neighborhood. Just a quiet prayer every morning for Him to fill up your heart and life that new day, so that His unselfish love might be reflected from you to your little world.

> The last rays of merciful light, the last message of mercy to be given to the world, is a revelation of [God's] character of love. The children of God are to manifest His glory. In their own life and character they are to reveal what the grace of God has done for them. (*Christ's Object Lessons*, pp. 415, 416.)

But then, that's what the Jesus Generation is all about.

I think of that letter C.S. Lewis once wrote about Seventh-day Adventists. In the little compilation, *Letters to an American Lady*, you'll discover an intriguing bit of trans-Atlantic correspondence from Lewis—one of the bright literary minds of this century, arguably the most famous Christian writer of the century, and considered by many to be one of the most articulate and persuasive proponents of Christianity in the twentieth century.

Lewis and a woman here in the United States began a long correspondence during the late 50s. They never met face to face. But after his death this anonymous woman gave the letters she had received from Lewis to a publisher, and thus the book.

While we don't have any of her letters, from the content of his letters to her you can surmise what she wrote to him.

Apparently she has had a favorable encounter with an Adventist somewhere in this country. Not knowing much about the members of this particular church herself, she writes to Lewis and asks his opinion of Adventists.

On October 26, 1962, a year before his death, Lewis wrote back: "What you say about the VII Day Adventists interests me extremely. If they have so much charity there must be something very right about them" (p. 109).

An anonymous woman bumps into an Adventist somewhere, sometime. And when she later tells the story to a world-renowned scholar, he muses back to her, "If they have so much charity there must be something very right about them."

"By this everyone will know that you are my disciples, if you have love for one another" (John 13:35). Jesus' quiet execution-eve declaration proves true, doesn't it? The Jesus Generation is the last generation to share His passion to love a lost world back to the Father.

Malcolm X and C. S. Lewis prove the veracity of these words:

> Now that Jesus has ascended to heaven, His disciples are His representatives among men, and *one of the most effective ways of winning souls to Him is in exemplifying His character in our daily life.* Our influence upon others depends not so much upon what we say as upon what we are. Men may combat and defy our logic, they may resist our appeals; but *a life of disinterested love is an argument they cannot gainsay.* A consistent life, characterized by the meekness of Christ, is a power in the world. (*The Desire of Ages*, pp. 141,142, emphasis supplied.)

For, "if they have so much charity there must be something very right about them."

So for all the Malcolm Xs and the C. S. Lewises and the anonymous American ladies that cross our paths and share our days, isn't now the right time for the unselfish love of Jesus to radiate from our marriages and our homes, from our offices and our professions, from our businesses and our hospitals, from our schools and our churches?

Let the record show that God has not raised up this end-time generation so they might draw the world to themselves. The evidence is clear—their prophetic mandate is to be the **Jesus** Generation. For it is when they lift *Him* up that His promise at last will come true: "And I, when I am lifted up from the earth, will draw all people to myself" (John 12:32).

A passion in crimson. A people of the cross. No wonder earth's last nightfall is lighted with the fire of Jesus in this generation.

"Be like Jesus, this my song, in the home and in the throng; be like Jesus all day long; I would be like Jesus."

It can be your song, too.